THE QUEST

THE
QUEST

THE DEFINITIVE GUIDE TO
FINDING BELONGING

DAN J. BERGER

Forbes | Books

Published by Forbes Books, Charleston, South Carolina.
An imprint of Advantage Media Group.

Forbes Books is a registered trademark, and the Forbes Books colophon is a trademark of Forbes Media, LLC.

Printed in the United States of America.

10 9 8 7 6 5 4 3 2 1

ISBN: 979-8-88750-116-1 (Hardcover)
ISBN: 979-8-88750-117-8 (eBook)

Library of Congress Control Number: 2024920911

Cover design by Lance Buckley.

This custom publication is intended to provide accurate information and the opinions of the author in regard to the subject matter covered. It is sold with the understanding that the publisher, Forbes Books, is not engaged in rendering legal, financial, or professional services of any kind. If legal advice or other expert assistance is required, the reader is advised to seek the services of a competent professional.

Since 1917, Forbes has remained steadfast in its mission to serve as the defining voice of entrepreneurial capitalism. Forbes Books, launched in 2016 through a partnership with Advantage Media, furthers that aim by helping business and thought leaders bring their stories, passion, and knowledge to the forefront in custom books. Opinions expressed by Forbes Books authors are their own. To be considered for publication, please visit **books.Forbes.com**.

To my mom, Roni,
for being the strongest woman I know and
for teaching me to never stop learning.

My loving wife, Jen,
who made me feel like I belong for the first time in my life.

My daughter, Sela,
I commit to always making you feel like you belong.

And, finally, to all the people who helped make Social Tables
become what I knew it could be. Thank you.

CONTENTS

STAGE II: BASECAMP

STAGE III: HIGH CAMP

STAGE IV: SUMMIT

STAGE I
TRAILHEAD

TRAILHEAD

CHAPTER 1
YOU DON'T BELONG EVERYWHERE

"The best view comes after the hardest climb."
—ANONYMOUS

Don't screw this up, I thought to myself as I stood in a circle of several new classmates.

Like most business schools in 2008, my class was 70 percent male. I assumed this meant there would be a great deal of sports talk, and my knowledge of the entire subject consisted of Knicks trivia from the 1990s. So, I spent the week before the start of the school year binging *SportsCenter*. I memorized key stats, learned about the pro teams, and studied the upcoming major league schedules. I even learned to hate Dan Snyder.

On the day school started, having completed my self-designed crash course, I was anxious to flex my newfound knowledge. Despite feeling nervous, I summoned the courage to engage another student. "Are you excited about RBG's debut?" I asked, mustering up all the confidence I could find in my being.

My question was met with an awkward smile as my classmate turned away to find someone else to talk to. Later, I realized I'd mixed up rising star quarterback Robert Griffin III ("RG3") with Supreme Court Justice Ruth Bader Ginsburg. So much for not screwing that up.

Even though I had made my best effort to belong, I'd messed it up. I felt like a fraud; this just wasn't my world. Despite the voracious preparation, my attempts to make conversation had blown up in my face. While it may seem insignificant, this moment in my life revealed a bigger issue—one that you might be able to relate to.

I was trying to fit in somewhere I didn't belong.

Belonging starts with knowing and accepting ourselves. This self-awareness lays the groundwork for discovering where and how we fit in the world. While my motivation to belong was sincere, I was inauthentic to myself and to others in how I tried to do it.

Recognizing our intrinsic social needs helps us choose the right opportunities for seeking belonging. Failing to do so sincerely, much like my experience, is a surefire way to experience rejection. And rejection can really hurt.

> **I was trying to fit in somewhere I didn't belong.**

At least I now understand the difference between authentically trying to belong versus trying to force it. I wish the same could be said for corporate America where fake attempts at belonging run rampant.

It's hard not to roll your eyes at HR teams' fervent attempts to ensure "everybody belongs." Slogans like "you belong" and "we belong here" are woven into marketing campaigns to instill a sense of connection and inclusion in consumers, but they often fall flat. The concept of belonging is so overused in marketing that even the Ad Council, the nonprofit responsible for distributing PSAs on behalf of the US government, has a major campaign dedicated to it.

Barclays Center, Brooklyn, New York

An unnamed Planet Fitness location

Similarly, the term *community* has become diluted. Nowadays, everything is labeled a community, from people who wear the same brand of clothing to subscribers of a YouTube channel. Like the ubiquitous belonging campaigns, these so-called communities claim to welcome everyone.

This over-inclusiveness presents a glaring problem: *if everyone belongs, no one belongs.*

One place you *can* be certain you belong is right here, right now. Picking up this book shows a commitment to self-improvement through personal exploration. You acknowledge that you have gaps in knowledge. These qualities show both intellectual curiosity *and* intellectual honesty. However, you're not alone—*every person* seeks to belong, whether they use that

> **If everyone belongs, no one belongs.**

term or not. Yet, I see very few people discussing what this term *actually* means or how to find belonging methodically.

I wrote this book to do exactly that.

ABOUT THIS BOOK

The Quest is a transformative process designed to help individuals enhance their sense of belonging. By aligning both our personality and environment with how we find belonging, our connection to the world becomes profoundly stronger. This journey shifts us from a state of passive existence to one of persistent joy.

Like any climb, our adventure is split into stages that represent distinct phases of our ascent. The completion of each stage is an accomplishment in and of itself. Achieving these milestones will be punctuated by simple exercises to zero in on how you find belonging and which belonging routes work best for you.

You are already at the first stage: **trailhead**. Like any good signpost, this stage previews the journey ahead and warns us of what will happen if we veer off the path. After a cursory review of topical research materials, I present a working definition of the word *belonging* and discuss why many admired authors have misled us about the issue. We will then explore our country's Belonging Crisis and develop a thesis on how to solve it (hint: you're already doing it by reading this book).

The second stage is **basecamp**. This is where we will pay homage to the forces outside of our control as we gear up for what awaits. Here you will take stock of who you are—what you can and can't change about yourself. You will get to know the different paths to belonging on the trek ahead, meet the different belonging archetypes, and select the one that works best for you.

The third stage is **high camp**, where you will prepare for the summit push. As with any climb, you need to acclimate a bit before you can head up, so we will settle down to explore all the different belonging paths at our disposal in more detail. You will complete this stage holding a container with all the activities that give you a sense of belonging.

The fourth and final stage is the **summit**. Unlike other climbs, however, you won't be descending. You'll be staying at the mountaintop. That's because, once you've summited *this* quest, you will have a clear understanding of your belonging needs. This clarity will last a lifetime. At the top, you will also scan the horizon to see your environment from above, enabling you to make changes that can directly impact how you find belonging going forward. I'll close by teaching you the five skills you can develop to keep improving your sense of belonging.

When you finish reading this book, it is my sincere hope that you will be equipped with all the knowledge and tools you need to claim your place in the world. As a direct result of our work, you will experience a state of persistent joy.

FOR ME, THIS SUBJECT IS PERSONAL

Adoption and Abandonment

My first experience with belonging-related trauma happened when I was in utero and my mentally ill biological mother made the decision to give me up for adoption just a few months into her pregnancy.[i] From that point on, she was biochemically communicating to me that I was not wanted.

---

i   Prenatal stress can influence a child's development by transmitting stress hormones like cortisol to the fetus.

This *primal wound,* a term coined by psychotherapist and author Nancy Verrier to describe the visceral pain adoptees feel, has left me feeling like I am bad, broken, and unworthy of love ever since.

I was adopted when I was five days old. At such a young age, adopted children often confuse their adoptive mother with their abandoning biological mother. The adoptive parents, especially the mom, wind up on the receiving end of the adoptee's resentment.[1]

This was my experience. During adolescence, as the sadness of losing my biological mom turned to rage, I directed a lot of it at my adoptive mother, severely mistreating her. As I've grown older, however, I've developed a great deal of empathy for what she endured. As a young woman, burdened by infertility, she had to spend ten years on the adoption waiting list. In fact, she had so little information about where she was in the queue that she kept baby products in the trunk of her car to be as ready as possible when the adoption agency called her with good news.

This long, treacherous wait led her to treat me as "special." This treatment resulted in a form of permissive parenting that neither established healthy boundaries for me nor introduced appropriate consequences for my actions. I was the baby meant for her. I've experienced similar treatment from others who have told me I'm lucky and that I should be grateful. All I took away from this toxic positivity, however, were high standards that I couldn't meet. These unreasonable expectations contributed to my negative self-talk. *When would the ruse that I'm unwanted end? When would the fraud I was per-petrating become exposed?*

Many adoptees experience this kind of deep-rooted belief that they are fundamentally flawed. It can lead them to feel undeserving of being cared for and burdened with a perpetual sense of guilt.

The abandonment I suffered at the hands of my bio-logical mom contributed heavily to my insecurities around attachment. In so many words, the parents that conceived me told me they didn't want me—that I didn't belong with them. Subconsciously I was programmed to believe I would always be left behind.

Divorce and Neglect

Around my second birthday, I experienced another belong-ing-related trauma: my adoptive parents divorced. Suddenly, the nuclear family I was a part of was split. My mom got full custody of me, and my dad got visitation rights, which he rarely exercised—and when he did, he was always late, rushed, or checked out. To make matters worse, when he remarried when I was five, he did not invite me to his wedding. This was the first signal of many over the years that I did not belong in the new family he was building.

To this day, I long for the love and attention of a masculine role model. Although my adoptive dad is nearly eighty and I know that the only way to heal from his neglect will come from within me, I still fantasize about the day he might come to me with an apology for being absent from my life. I miss the father I never had.

Immigration and Isolation

Adding to the laundry list of childhood traumas I endured, my mom moved us to New York City when I was eight to live with my future stepdad. Moving at this age made me what sociologist Rubén Rumbaut calls a "one-and-a-half generation immigrant" living in the "cultural borderland." This term describes children who relocate at a young age. They embrace some of their new cultural norms but question others. The overwhelming cultural shock I experienced had a profound effect on my sense of self.

Immigration further wounded my fragile sense of belonging. I didn't belong fully to either America or Israel. I felt like an outsider wherever I went. As a result, I have struggled to this day with defining my nationality. *Am I Israeli-American or American-Israeli? Why is it that in America I feel like an Israeli, and in Israel I feel like an American?*

While all these traumas of neglect, abandonment, and isolation strengthened my resilience and adaptability, they also caused me chronic stress. As I grew older, I started seeing a pattern—I never truly had a secure sense of belonging. This emptiness would eventually serve as a spark for my entrepreneurial endeavors.

HEALTHY AND UNHEALTHY COPING

When my friend Elad invited me to his wedding in 2008, anxiety took over. It was the first American wedding I had ever been invited to, and the only thought racing through my mind was *What will I talk to the people at my table about?*

As a web designer at the time, my mind immediately jumped to a tech solution. This is when the idea for Social Tables was born. Keeping the anxious guest's needs in mind, the app I envisioned would allow every guest to browse the Facebook profiles of their tablemates to learn a little bit about them, their professions, their interests, and so on in order to jumpstart the evening's conversations. A digital social table.

The solution, I imagined, would remove some of the stressful guesswork from socializing. It would allow me to engineer my way through the anxiety by controlling who I talked to and the topics we discussed. This, in turn, would prevent someone from ignoring me, because I would ignore them first.

As I reflect on the real motivation behind my venture, the writing is on the wall. Socially engineering situations is a trauma response I had developed from the abandonment I experienced growing up. It led me to develop defense mechanisms to shield myself from the hurt, and this app idea was the latest such innovation.

A second, more subversive and, up until recently, subconscious tactic I used to manage my fear of abandonment was denigrating others in my head. Whenever I would not be praised in a group setting or receive attention in a social situation, I would crawl into a dark mental space and view those around me as inferior or not deserving of my time. This behavior, I now know, stems from very low self-esteem.

These two coping mechanisms provided temporary security, but they also hindered my ability to sit with my feelings and find healthy ways to grow from my abandonment issues. The irony of these tactics was that they were having the opposite effect to what I had intended. They further isolated me. I stunted the growth of certain social skills, such as empathy and intimacy, and limited my exposure to worthwhile people.

Devoid of these interpersonal skills, I was not developing the adult relationships I needed to feel a sense of belonging. Without them, I was only experiencing superficial connections, friendships, and romance. Underneath it all, I was still an abandoned boy who was never given the chance to fit in.

THE BREAKTHROUGHS

Social Tables, the little-engine-that-could seating chart app grew to become one of the most recognized software platforms in the events and hospitality industry. Its dynamic culture unlocked my sense of belonging for the nine years I was at the helm.

It was here where colleagues-turned-friends lifted my spirits, company events gave me a feeling of togetherness, industry conferences made me feel important, and press articles told me we were special. But after selling the company in 2018, it was all gone. And so too was my sense of belonging. For the decade I ran the company, I didn't realize the belonging I had was temporary. It would only last as long as my tenure. Reflecting on this really special time in my life, I had a major breakthrough.

I realized that I never had a personal sense of belonging to begin with. Instead of finding connection through typical avenues like family, romantic partnerships, or spirituality, I relied on fruitless endeavors such as workaholism, chronic dating, and nihilism, which only served to fight off connection rather than find it. I learned that personal belonging is foundational; it must come before professional (i.e., career) belonging. While personal belonging stays with us unconditionally, professional belonging only lasts as long as an employee contract. In other words, when we have belonging in our personal life, we have a safety net that no job can replace.

This insight came during the COVID-19 pandemic. As the world shut down, I found myself with zero obligations and a lot of time on my hands. For eighteen months after the start of the pandemic and guided mostly by my intuition, I made it my personal quest to seek that sense of belonging that I craved but never truly had.

This journey started when I read entrepreneur Bob Buford's book *Halftime: Moving from Success to Significance*. It inspired me to create space after the sale of my business to figure out my next move—my halftime. *If the first half of my life ended the moment I sold my company, then instead of jumping into the second half—whatever it might be—I should take some time to figure things out*, I thought to myself. Maybe a newer purpose would emerge.

In the year and a half that made up my halftime, I gave my life a radical makeover. It started with a 2,500-mile road trip that took me from the East Coast, where I had spent the past thirty years of my life, to the Pacific Northwest, where I had never set foot before. Once settled in my new home, I spent a year focused on self-care and personal discovery.

Embarking on numerous healing journeys, I delved into my childhood traumas with renewed determination. I embraced new interests, explored intriguing hobbies, and took bold risks that once intimidated me. In reevaluating my friendships, I deepened bonds and formed new ones with those who resonated with my personal renaissance. I discovered and invested in a home that suited my new adult lifestyle in a neighborhood that felt right. I became actively involved in philanthropic and community activities. Navigating the dating scene, I sought a compatible partner while broadening my perspectives through literature and writing. Mindfulness practices, such as meditation and neurofeedback, granted me a balance and clarity I had long yearned for. Prioritizing my physical health, I finally underwent a few overdue surgeries, engaged a personal trainer, and began consulting a nutritionist.

Through this meticulous yet unplanned process, I discovered an inspiring purpose for the second half of my life that I felt would help me achieve significance: helping others find their sense of belonging—something I never felt I possessed or deserved myself—by sharing my journey.

Just because I found belonging one way, however, doesn't mean others will find it the same way. I decided to codify my process in way that can work for anyone. One problem remained: I had to battle my nasty impostor syndrome.

WHY ME

I quickly realized that my self-doubt is exactly why I'm the perfect person for the task. That I have never experienced belonging but have instead grappled with isolation, loneliness, and feeling like an outsider makes me the perfect person to help others find belonging.

In order to give my new mission credibility, I had to become an expert on the subject. I immersed myself in the body of "belonging literature,"

> **Just because I found belonging one way, however, doesn't mean others will find it the same way.**

reading hundreds of articles, books, and academic papers. It was important for me to learn the science of belonging and empirically validate my intuitive experiences.

But why dedicate an entire book to *my* journey and its lessons? Aren't there already enough self-proclaimed experts dissecting the concept of belonging? I've questioned my motivations more times than I can count. I've often recalled my friend Ken's incredulous inquiries about why I continue to embark on new ventures when I could easily rest on my laurels and enjoy the fruits of my labor.

The answer is simple—if even a handful of readers resonate with this book and are encouraged to undertake their own journeys to find belonging, then every word written has fulfilled its purpose.

In writing *The Quest*, I've come to realize that while its "why" is a fundamental human drive to feel a sense of belonging, its "how" remains elusive for so many. This book aims to articulate this second part. It's a guidebook for anyone seeking a sense of place, identity, and meaningful connection.

> It's a guidebook for anyone seeking a sense of place, identity, and meaningful connection.

So, whether you're after a total "glow up" of your sense of belonging or feeling just a little bit lonely, know that the answers you seek are within reach. *The Quest* will be your companion on this very personal journey, offering research, insights, exercises, customized advice, and personal anecdotes. And, of course, plenty of encouragement and reassurance every step of the way.

CHAPTER 2

NO SHORTCUTS TO THE TOP

*"We suggest that belongingness can be almost
as compelling a need as food."*
—ROY F. BAUMEISTER AND MARK R. LEARY

"You're not a good culture fit," the president of the local chapter of the Young Presidents' Organization, a global business association I had been a part of for nearly a decade, told me over the phone one evening. He was asking me to resign.

My heart sank to my stomach. Reaching for the victim card, I asked myself, *How can they do this to me?* I was respected and liked at my previous chapter. I even received the Member of the Year award a couple of years prior in a different chapter. *How did I screw up?*

I thought I was doing everything right: engaging with fellow members, being helpful where I could be, and attending every event on the social calendar.

After we ended the conversation, I went on the offensive. I called members of the executive committee to debrief them and ask for help. I reached out to friends in the chapter to plead my case. And when things felt hopeless, I started wondering whether it was because my identity as a left-leaning Jewish New Yorker was not the right match for the relatively homogenous group.

Over the coming weeks, I stewed in my anger and started considering my legal options. *Were the chapter's bylaws violated? Was I being discriminated against?*

As my ego subsided, reality set in. They simply didn't like me. *I don't need them to feel like I belong*, I thought to myself. I felt a sense of relief as I reclaimed my agency.

Belonging is not just a feeling. It's a story. A story of continuous fit. One day you can feel like you belong, and the next you can be crushed by not feeling it at all. No one is to blame, not even ourselves. As we change, as others change, and as everything around us changes, it's only natural for the feeling of belonging to shift as well.

Unlike typical feelings, such as impatience, gratitude, and sadness, belonging is not always up to you. While there are ways to feel a sense of belonging without being social, which we will explore in later chapters, its primary paths require people. And anything that involves other people is messy. They add an element of uncertainty to the equation.

> One day you can feel like you belong, and the next you can be crushed by not feeling it at all.

As I write these words, belonging is trending. It's all the rage in "pop-psych" circles. It's a topic that is commonly mentioned in self-help resources, promoted by HR consultants, and especially bastardized in the wellness industry. We can't avoid it, and every overused mention increasingly dilutes its meaning. But what *exactly* do I mean when I talk about "belonging"?

Let's start with the obvious and see what the *Oxford Advanced Learner's Dictionary* says:

> *Belonging is "the feeling of being comfortable and happy in a particular situation or with a particular group of people and being treated as a full member of the group."*[2]

As we explore the modern fascination with belonging, it's crucial to ground our understanding in its foundational concepts.

A FUNDAMENTAL NEED

This journey takes us back to 1943 when psychologist Abraham H. Maslow introduced the Hierarchy of Needs, a groundbreaking model for understanding human motivation. Today, his famous pyramid is widely recognized and accepted as a framework for explaining both our motivations and their order of operation in the human psyche. You can't meet your safety needs, for example, if your physiological needs are not being met.

Maslow's Hierarchy of Needs (1943)[ii, 3]

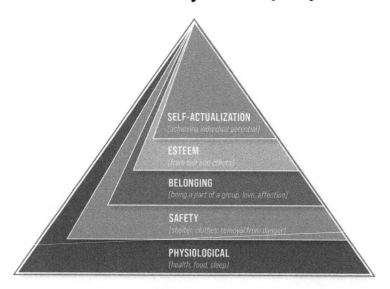

SELF-ACTUALIZATION
(achieving individual potential)

ESTEEM
(from self and others)

BELONGING
(being a part of a group, love, affection)

SAFETY
(shelter, clothes, removal from danger)

PHYSIOLOGICAL
(health, food, sleep)

Maslow placed belonging in the middle of the pyramid, defining it as the deep need for close relationships and a sense of connection.[4] Sandwiched between the need for physical safety (i.e., shelter, clothes, removal from danger) and esteem (e.g., sense of self-worth from oneself and from others), he visually showed us belonging's critical importance to the human experience.

> Maslow placed belonging in the middle of the pyramid, defining it as the deep need for close relationships and a sense of connection.

---

ii   In 1963, Maslow revisited his pyramid, adding three more levels to the original: cognitive and aesthetic needs (between esteem and self-actualization), and a top level, transcendence, above self-actualization.

In 2010, a group of prominent researchers led by psychologist Douglas T. Kenrick offered several revisions to Maslow's original model. They found that self-actualization, once considered a distinct need, overlaps with esteem and mating needs. This overlap is because achieving one's full potential often requires both self-worth and meaningful relationships. Instead, they proposed that *parenting* take the top spot, with *mate retention* and *mate acquisition* below it.[5]

An Updated Hierarchy of Fundamental Human Motives (2010)[6]

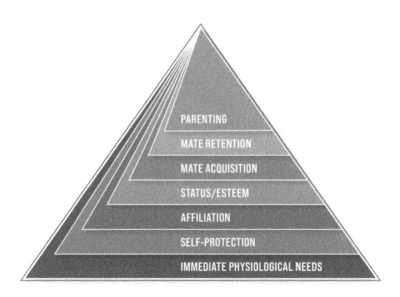

The term *belonging* was replaced with *affiliation*, but neither the spirit of the psychological need nor its spot in third position from the bottom was changed. The researchers defined affiliation as the need for social connections that offer mutual benefits, such as emotional support as well as the sharing of tangible resources like time and information. These connections usually take place within a protective group environment where they are enhanced through reciprocal interactions.

A VIRTUOUS CYCLE

Between the release of Maslow's pyramid and that of Kenrick's, the definition of belonging among social scientists itself evolved.

In the mid-1960s, belonging was defined as involvement in a social system where individuals feel they are an indispensable and integral part of the group.[7] Thirty years later, the definition was refined to make belonging a two-way street, requiring "a person's fit within a group and a feeling that one is a necessary part of the group."[8] The term *fit* is critical here, as it implies that the individual is compatible with the group and vice versa.

Belonging creates a positive feedback loop. When we have enjoyable social experiences, we want to seek out more of them and feel like we belong. This constant validation from our environment fosters a genuine sense of belonging, encompassing both emotions and experiences. The loop is reinforced.

> **The term *fit* is critical here, as it implies that the individual is compatible with the group and vice versa.**

Belonging Is a Feedback Loop

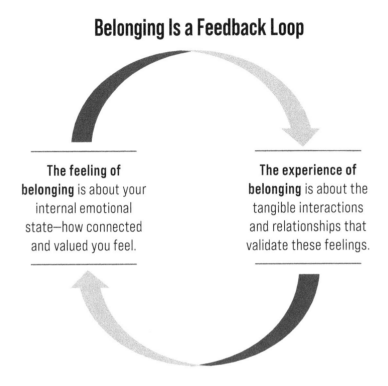

The feeling of belonging is about your internal emotional state—how connected and valued you feel.

The experience of belonging is about the tangible interactions and relationships that validate these feelings.

This virtuous cycle has significant health implications as well. Feelings of belonging contribute to our well-being[9] as well as our life purpose.[10] Meanwhile, feelings of not belonging contribute to mental and physical health problems, as well as reduced longevity.[11]

OUR WORKING DEFINITION

After a thorough review of the literature, I can definitively tell you that there is no agreement on a modern definition of the word *belonging* in the field of psychology as of this writing.[12]

Taking into consideration all the research, history, and ideas, I decided to add my own definition to the mix: *the sense of fit within a social system where an individual feels accepted and essential, while experiencing moments that reinforce these feelings.* Here is a breakdown of each of the components in this definition.

- **Sense of fit.** The alignment between the involved parties (e.g., person and group).

- **Social system.** The various social structures, relationships, and environments one can belong to.

- **Acceptance.** The individual feels seen for who they are, included, and respected.

- **Essential.** The individual feels they're a valued part of the system.

- **Reinforcement.** The system regularly reciprocates belonging feelings through the experience of participating in it.

There is an important distinction I'd like to raise between a state of belonging and a sense of belonging. The former suggests the feeling is ephemeral in nature and can change as often as several times per day. The latter refers to a more persistent, stable, and lasting feeling.[iii] This latter definition is our goal on *The Quest*.

Even referring to belonging as a "sense" is significant and purposeful. This terminology implies that belonging is an

---

iii   Some social scientists refer to this state as *belongingness*.

intuitive experience, allowing us to deeply feel when we are included or, conversely, when we are marginalized or othered.[13]

WHAT CAME FIRST, BELONGING OR IDENTITY?

Exploring the building blocks of belonging naturally brings us to the topic of identity. The relationship between belonging and identity is intertwined, much like the classic "chicken or the egg" question.

Is it our sense of belonging that shapes our identity, or is it our identity that determines where we belong? They overlap and reinforce each other, making it difficult to determine which comes first.

Identity becomes apparent in children when they start recognizing themselves as separate individuals. As they grow and social dynamics become more prevalent, their identities are shaped dramatically by their peer groups. When children become adults, their identity and sense of belonging become less dependent on each other and more interconnected, constantly reinforcing one another.[iv]

Identity is about understanding and expressing one's unique individuality. This manifests in our affiliations, family structure, profession, places we live, and so on. While our *identity* provides us with labels, *belonging* provides us with an emotional connection to these labels.

---

iv   This is, of course, different across cultures, where group identity may take precedence over individual identity. For this reason, I am only talking about American culture, where individual identity trumps group identity.

Even though I've identified as Jewish-American, I never really felt like I belonged to that cultural segment of American society. I had the label but not the group affiliation. It was through my involvement in different Jewish organizations and connecting with other Jews that I began to grasp the interplay between identity and belonging.

As I engaged more deeply with the Jewish community, I started to see my own identity more clearly and felt a profound sense of belonging that had previously eluded me. This experience illustrated how belonging to a group reinforces our identity by reflecting our self-expression—acting as a social mirror.

> While our *identity* provides us with labels, *belonging* provides us with an emotional connection to these labels.

On the other hand, our identity may drive our desire to belong to groups that resonate with our self-perception. This is where we often find tension. Sometimes, the need to belong can be so overwhelming that it compels individuals to either exaggerate or suppress parts of their identity to fit in.

Overemphasizing identity, especially as it relates to race, gender, sex, and sexuality, argues political scientist Yascha Mounk in *The Identity Trap*, can lead to the societal dysfunction and polarization we have been witnessing throughout our country as of late.

MYTH-BUSTING THE GURUS

Despite the fact that the concept of belonging has emerged as a cottage industry, I've not yet encountered a comprehensive guide to finding it. Worse, many writers—from best-selling authors to self-help gurus—oversimplify the concept.

Brené Brown, clinical social worker by profession and the author of *Braving the Wilderness*, defines belonging as "the innate human desire to be a part of something larger than us."[14] To meet this need, she explains, people are often inauthentic because they're trying so desperately to fit in. Brown abstracts a new concept she calls *true belonging*, which she refers to as a "spiritual practice." She says that when you are your true self, you can "find sacredness either by being a part of something or standing alone."[15] Helping people develop the courage to stand alone seems to be her primary goal.[16]

While Brown is right that belonging starts with the self and is helped by a spiritual connection to the broader universe, I disagree with her in two ways. First, while I believe that belonging can be partially found through spirituality, I think suggesting it can only be achieved through spiritual means is misleading. Such a suggestion overlooks the varied paths people use to find belonging.

Second, Brown's assertion that one can find belonging by "standing alone" misrepresents the multiple understandings of belonging I presented earlier. Due to its nature as a sentiment that stems directly from social interaction, it is simply not possible for it to arise from isolation.

People sometimes search for belonging by going on a solo journey, like what Elizabeth Gilbert describes in her memoir *Eat, Pray, Love*. Despite the enriching and enjoyable nature of such walkabouts, sabbaticals remain inaccessible to most due to time constraints and financial limitations. Although travel might offer a temporary sense of belonging, it cannot provide the traveler with a sustainable belonging source. Journeying alone, as Gilbert recommends, or being in the proverbial wilderness, as Brown suggests, can be the start of a quest for belonging—but it cannot be its ultimate goal.

Renowned self-help author Eckhart Tolle also touches on belonging in his books on spirituality. One of his major points is that one may find peace by realizing who they are at their deepest level instead of rearranging the circumstances of their life. The same critique of Brown applies here as well: it's not only difficult but also unhelpful for those not at this level of spirituality. Folks like us want the playbook. We want to know how to get there and not what it feels like *once* you're there.

Without embarking on a quest involving intense self-discovery and a lot of trial and error, authors like Brown, Gilbert, and Tolle inadvertently promote *spiritual bypassing*. Coined by clinical psychologist

John Welwood, this is the use of spiritual concepts to shirk the actual developmental work.[17]

We won't ignore unresolved issues. Our quest will sequentially address all the building blocks to help you find belonging. There are no shortcuts or hacks. You have to put in the work. Address the deep-rooted issues that keep you from overcoming loneliness. Find the belonging you deserve, and it will bring you a joyful life.

CHAPTER 3

CRISIS AROUND THE CORNER

"The experience of loneliness and isolation is just as toxic [as asbestos and cigarettes] when prolonged."
—GEOFFREY L. COHEN

My mom and I moved to NYC when I was eight, during the summer between third and fourth grade. As an immigrant, I have been othered many times over, but nothing compared to the loneliness I felt when we first moved to the States. I was extremely nervous about being the new kid, especially since nearly all my classmates had known each other for several years. One moment in particular is burned in my memory, as it captures my deep sense of aloneness at that time.

It was the first week of school, and the choir was holding tryouts. It seemed like the cool thing to do, so I decided to give it a shot. For reasons still unknown to me, the music teacher selected only twenty-two of my twenty-four class-mates during the tryouts. A fellow immigrant, Eugene, and I were the only ones who didn't make the cut. To make matters worse, every Friday Eugene and I had to sit in a classroom alone while the rest of the class went to choir practice down the hall. Through the walls, we could hear them harmonizing. It was humiliating.

I am certain you have memories like this one—sad stories of how you were treated unfairly before you had the capacity to stand up for yourself. These experiences of exclusion are not just personal anecdotes but reflections of a broader societal issue.

As we navigate through life, the feelings of disconnection we faced as children often follow us into adulthood. These feelings are magnified by the changing dynamics within our communities and throughout our country. Technological advancement and social media only compound this problem.

AN EPIDEMIC OF LONELINESS

A silent, intensifying epidemic has been brewing in our country for seventy-five years.

It started with two seemingly unrelated events in the 1950s. The first was the proliferation of television, further secluding families by moving entertainment indoors. The second was suburban development, spreading families across expansive geographic areas and reducing intra-community engagement.

This epidemic continued throughout the second half of the twentieth century. There was a decline in organized religion, erosion of work-life boundaries, and fading trust in institutions. American society was greatly affected by the results, leading to a decrease in civic engagement, community-meeting participation, and informal socializing. These trends weakened the fabric of social bonds and eroded the sense of community.

In his influential book *Bowling Alone*, renowned political scientist Robert Putnam referred to this phenomenon as a decline in *social capital*.[18] Unfortunately, this epidemic has only picked up steam. The meteoric rise of social media in the 2010s made us more *isolated*, while the COVID-19 pandemic in the early 2020s made us more *insular*.

This epidemic is best described as a sense of pervasive loneliness. It is silent and multigenerational. Much like a mutating virus, it is resistant to most remedies. Every age group, socioeconomic class, and demographic is affected.

We often think of loneliness as something associated with the elderly. Something pitiable yet inevitable with the passage of time—spouses and friends pass, kids get older, and our health fails us. It should shock us all then that young adults are two times more likely to be lonely than seniors.[19]

The extent of loneliness among our youth led US Surgeon General Vivek Murthy to issue a rare public health advisory in 2021, warning of "persistent feelings of sadness or hopelessness" among young people.[20] He has since promulgated this concern each year.[21] This isn't just a wild theory; several troubling trends support Murthy's concern. While the COVID-19 pandemic exacerbated the issue, self-reported feelings of loneliness had been swelling well before the pandemic began.

Men in Crisis

It's no secret that due to a combination of factors, men have been impacted by loneliness the most.[22] The discourse on gender identity and toxic masculinity has turned the very notion of traditional masculinity on its head. The shift in gender roles, with women advancing professionally and online dating altering traditional courting, has led some men to feel marginalized and overlooked.

Furthermore, the public discussion around diversity, equity, and inclusion has led some men to feel penalized for their identity, irrespective of the fairness of these initiatives. Various factors contribute to men generally having fewer friendships compared to women, particu- larly lacking emotionally supportive relationships.[23] This lack of support is a factor in the grim reality that men not only have shorter average lifespans but also higher rates of deaths of despair (including suicide, drug overdoses, and alcohol-related liver disease). In essence, many men feel marginalized and pushed toward insignificance.

Nearly four out of five eighteen- to twenty-two-year-olds reported feeling lonely in 2019.[24] College life, once a bastion of socialization, has seen a marked decline in student interaction. Today's students are more disengaged, less resilient, and struggle with more mental health problems such as anxiety, trauma, depression, self-esteem issues, learning disabilities, and suicidal ideation.[25]

Younger Americans Are More Alone[26]

Share of Americans who reported feeling lonely in 2019

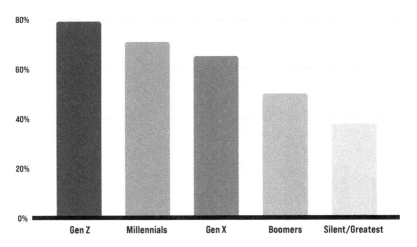

These issues have downstream implications. More Americans are living alone than ever before. In fact, more than one in four Americans lives alone, a fifty-year high.[27] While merely living alone doesn't mean someone is necessarily lonely, it may indicate that they are isolated.

More Americans Are Living Alone[28]

One-Person Households as a Percentage of
All US Households: 1940–2020

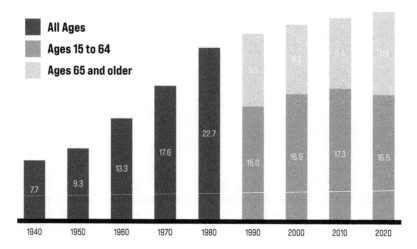

Note: Alaska and Hawaii are not included in the US totals for 1940 and 1950.

The feeling of loneliness is described as an evolutionary warning system because, historically, being isolated in nature meant certain death. Today's modern world is not much different. In their groundbreaking book on the harmful effects of loneliness, neuroscientist John T. Cacioppo and author William Patrick present research showing how loneliness can be as harmful as physical pain. Apart from its mental health implications, loneliness can weaken our cardiovascular functions and immune system. [29]

FROM EPIDEMIC TO CRISIS

During the Progressive Era (1890s to1920s) most Americans felt a powerful sense of belonging. People were passionate and purposeful in their engagement with public life. This period was characterized by ambitious new types of civic associations, such as member organizations, labor unions, and social reforms driven by a new generation of civic leaders.[30] This was a time of significant positive social, economic, and political change in the US, thanks in part to our shared belonging.[31]

Today, due to our hyper-individualistic nature, this type of societal engagement is hard to imagine. It feels counterintuitive to how everyone around us lives, jostling to be seen and given space for their idiosyncrasy. This narcissism compounds loneliness by undermining genuine emotional connections. It diminishes empathy while increasing social isolation. This has turned our challenges into structural issues, leading to a crisis of belonging.

As transportation secretary Pete Buttigieg said during his 2019 presidential campaign, "Right now, there are a lot of lines being drawn about who gets to be American. And it speaks to a bigger crisis of belonging in this country."[32]

Buttigieg saw a unifying opportunity in this crisis: "[The] yearning for belonging

> **"Right now, there are a lot of lines being drawn about who gets to be American. And it speaks to a bigger crisis of belonging in this country."**

can either be the thing that divides us, because we find belonging in whatever tribe we align with … or we tap into something deeper, which is the fact that [we're] not that different."[33]

COMMUNITY > TRIBE

Despite Buttigieg's appeal to our shared humanity, things have not changed. America remains deeply divided. Across the political spectrum, individuals feel that others—whether fellow citizens or prospective Americans—do not belong. This sense of exclusion is reinforced by arbitrary lines drawn based on self-serving agendas rather than shared values. It's the difference between tribalism and community.

While tribalism may seem to give us a sense of belonging, it's actually the "dark twin of community," writes American cultural and political commentator David Brooks.[34] Tribalism is a connection based on ignorance and shared hatred while community is a connection based on fellowship, cooperation, and mutual affection. Tribalism has unfortunately led many people in our society to join radical groups and lean into questionable fringe philosophies. It's manipulating their legitimate needs for belonging and sincere desires for connection.

This manipulation of belonging needs can have deadly consequences. David Koresh's followers, the cult involved in the Waco siege, belonged, and they died in pursuit of belonging. Jim Jones's nine hundred followers, who committed a mass suicide, belonged, and together they drank the cyanide-laced Kool-Aid that fatally poisoned them. These extreme examples illustrate the dangerous power of tribalism.

The division caused by tribalism is often exacerbated by politicians who cast mindless blame on their opponents, each claiming the other side is the source of society's woes. This tactic distracts the public, manipulating

Tribalism is a connection based on ignorance and shared hatred while community is a connection based on fellowship, cooperation, and mutual affection.

perceptions and deepening feelings of alienation and loneliness. Tragically, these sinister strategies are not only divisive but deliberately employed to foster a state of anomie.

And they are indescribably effective.

AN AUTOCRAT'S FAVORITE WEAPON

Warnings about the societal dangers of loneliness were raised more than a century ago. In her book *The Origins of Totalitarianism*, political theorist and philosopher Hannah Arendt argues that mass loneliness is a fundamental ingredient for totalitarianism.

Totalitarianism is a political system where a centralized autocratic regime seeks total control over all aspects of public and private life. According to Arendt, autocrats often exploit loneliness to garner support.[35]

Loneliness can make people feel disconnected and alienated from society, conjuring a longing for community. Autocrats take advantage of this by offering a sense of belonging to those who feel isolated. This belonging is often based on shared hatred or fear of a common enemy, such as a particular ethnic or religious group, political party, or even physical characteristics.

Once autocrats create a sense of belonging among their followers, they use it to build a loyal base of support that is unlikely to challenge or question their authority. The fear of being punished for dissenting ideology creates a chilling effect, pushing the masses to fall in line. History is rife with such examples.

Stalin used mass purges and propaganda to foster a climate of fear and dependency, where loyalty to the state was the only safe harbor against being labeled an enemy—or worse, facing exile or execution. Hitler rallied a fractured and disillusioned populace around a nationalist and xenophobic ideology, creating a cohesive identity that targeted Jews and other minorities as external threats, thus uniting the majority through common foes. He promoted the idea of a *Volksgemeinschaft*, a people's community, which promised to unite the "racially pure" Germans as a single collective entity.

Similar campaigns are happening throughout the world today. The Kim dynasty in North Korea isolates citizens from each other and the outside world, creating a controlled environment where loyalty to its dictatorship is positioned as the only source of community and security. The Chinese government labels the Uyghur population as a security threat, fostering Han Chinese solidarity and justifying repressive measures for societal protection.

The misuse of loneliness by morally bankrupt leaders and corrupt governments transforms it into a weapon of mass destruction.

THE ANTIDOTE TO LONELINESS

Loneliness became a matter of medical responsibility due to COVID-19. Society suffered a paradigm shift to social distancing seemingly overnight. We all faced uncertainty amid forced separation as authorities prescribed lockdowns. The Belonging Crisis that previously affected the most vulnerable among us now spread throughout society.

The misuse of loneliness by morally bankrupt leaders and corrupt governments transforms it into a weapon of mass destruction.

Many people lost everyday interactions that made them feel alive. They couldn't commute, visit their usual coffee shops, or study in libraries. They lost regular rituals that shaped their lives, like playing sports, visiting friends, or doing other outdoor activities. Their work environments shifted as they stopped mingling with colleagues and holding face-to-face meetings.

That said, there was a silver lining. The pandemic served as a much-needed wake-up call for many. Most of us didn't realize we lacked a sense of belonging until our world came to a screeching halt. At that moment, we reclaimed our lives due to what I refer to as the *Great Realization*. In droves, we resigned from our jobs, packed up our homes, and set sail for unchartered waters to find greater meaning in our lives. Without knowing it, we were seeking a feeling of harmony and purpose within our environment. As a result, we returned to our human nature and learned that belonging is the antidote to loneliness.

If loneliness is the problem, belonging is the solution.

A BOTTOM-UP SOLUTION

Imagine a world where every person feels a sense of belonging. Social settings buzz as people enjoy the company of friends and colleagues. Couples have stable and loving relationships. People work with greater intention and enjoy financial and personal fulfillment as a result. They dedicate their free time to pursuing hobbies that bring them joy. This leads to less wasted time, resources, and effort. Above all, this increases global compassion as individuals become more mindful of themselves and one another.

> **If loneliness is the problem, belonging is the solution.**

This description is no fairy tale. It is within our grasp. But where do we start?

Unfortunately, there is no National Bureau for Belonging. Schools aren't teaching it as a skill. And certainly, despite what the latest investor-backed start-ups may have you believe, technology won't save us from our collective loneliness.[36]

Americans shared a greater sense of connection and community a century ago during the Progressive Era, and I am confident we can return to that. But what worked then won't necessarily work now. We've been served a layer cake of loneliness, and we can't seem to catch a break. The inward shift of the American experience seventy-five years ago has proliferated significantly. It has been compounded by counterproductive individuality, addictive technology, an isolating pandemic, and polarizing tribalism.

I believe that, unlike the top-down approach to belonging that worked in the early twentieth century, the next wave will have to come from within. The solution will start from the bottom up, with each person embarking on their own personal quest to authentically belong.

This is what we're committing to as we forge ahead past the trailhead.

> **The solution will start from the bottom up, with each person embarking on their own personal quest to authentically belong.**

STAGE II
BASECAMP

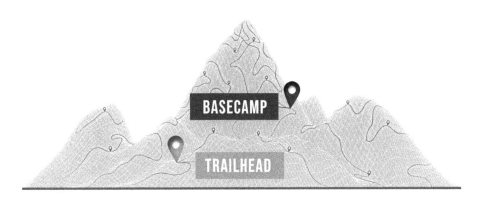

BASECAMP

TRAILHEAD

CHAPTER 4
SURRENDERING TO THE JOURNEY

*"Joy doesn't fade. To live with joy is to live
with wonder, gratitude, and hope."*
—DAVID BROOKS

"You're broken," says Chuck, a self-made multimillionaire who owned and operated the largest independent moving company in the US.

Little did I know, those two words would change my life forever.

His terse message was a response to a somber update I had shared about my personal life. He was one of my role models, so when he spoke, I listened. *You are broken.*

Strangely, I felt content being called broken. In my mind, a broken thing couldn't be fixed, which meant I could finally stop pretending I was fine. Over the next six years, I pondered those words, mindlessly taking them at face value. *I'm broken*, I'd remind myself whenever I needed to rationalize unbecoming behavior.

Then, in the summer of 2022, I went on a guided psilocybin journey. It was then that I made peace with my state of brokenness. Taking medicinal mushrooms with a therapeutic goal is different from doing so recreationally. There is a lot of attention placed on your mindset and environment.

Before I went on my journey, my guide led me through several sessions to help me refine my mindset. My aim was to develop "self-acceptance and self-love," something many people with my type of traumas struggle with. There was a meticulously crafted physical environment for the journey. Before an expansive window overlooking a breathtaking forested landscape, my guide carefully placed a comfortable mattress. The mat was surrounded by speakers that even the most discerning audiophile would revere.

After imbibing the medicine, I lay down, my body protected with a blanket to keep me snug. An eye mask covered my eyes, allowing me to turn completely inward. I gave in to the moment for the next five hours, while a carefully curated playlist provided a soothing soundtrack.

One of the most vivid visuals I had during my journey took place at the bottom of a pit. A closed wicker basket sat beside me, but I caught glimpses of faint light streaming through its weaves and gaps. My intuition told me this basket contained my traumas. I feared the light was an illusion, expecting darkness in its place. I was frightened, but I had to press on. Summoning courage, I lifted the lid to look inside.

Upon closer inspection, I was stunned to find pure, radiating light. The darkness was nowhere to be found. I felt a profound and sudden shift within me, one I can only describe as instant neuroplasticity. The traumatic experiences of abandonment, betrayal, and disappointment—once too overwhelming to address—now appeared as sources of strength and self-awareness. At that moment, I allowed myself to accept these traumas without judgment.

This experience taught me an invaluable lesson:

Broken things can be put back together.

Chuck was right about me being broken, but that was just *another part* of my story. Yes, my traumas scarred me, but in order to recover, I had to acknowledge them as an integral part of my being.

Acknowledging and comprehending our identities and past traumas is essential for feeling like we belong. This is reminiscent of the Stoics' philosophy, which was based entirely on one concept: *know thyself.* The Stoics believed that by becoming clear and unbiased we would have access to universal reason.

At **basecamp**, where we will prepare for and plan The Quest, this is our main priority. To know ourselves, we must first understand our spiritual orientation, which, at a minimum, will give us solace when shit happens and, at its highest form, may give us a sense of purpose. Next, we need a framework for keeping track of all the different methods we can use to find belonging. Finally, we need to get to know ourselves a little more intimately so that we know which belonging routes work for us.

Let's gear up.

FROM NIHILISM TO SPIRITUALITY

After he told me I was broken, Chuck suggested I partake in the *Hoffman Process*, a residential week-long therapeutic retreat. The program aims to address negative love patterns inherited through family lineage. Our parents pass down certain patterns to us, which they inherited from their parents and so on. It was through this experience that I learned how to be spiritual.

While spirituality may seem a given to some of you, I had been a proud atheist for most of my life leading up to Hoffman. To be frank, I was a total nihilist. I didn't follow any religion or have any spiritual beliefs. Furthermore, I believed that my actions—or lack thereof—had no significance at all. I felt no purpose beyond the present moment and would often refer to my infinitesimally small existence in the universe to prove my point.

My outlook shifted completely after going through the Hoffman Process. This approach helps people identify and address inherited negative behaviors, enabling them to make conscious choices and break free from compulsions. One negative pattern Hoffman cautions against is disparaging spirituality. This was something my mom had done through-out my life, and I adopted her approach as my worldview. She had a habit of laughing at other people's spiritual connections. Rather than giving me the freedom to discover spirituality on my own, she transmitted this pattern to me.

Consequently, I never envisioned myself as anything but an atheist. I didn't understand that I was parroting my mom's belief system without considering how unhelpful and limiting it had been in my life. The pessimistic outlook I had adopted was unintentionally robbing me of one of the paths to belonging.

Once I realized that my (dis)belief was inherited, I saw that I had always held a belief in a higher power and that the discomfort I experienced was related to the word *God*. Wisdom gleaned from an interview with Rabbi Steve Leder on Elise Loehnen's podcast, *Pulling the Thread*, may help you unravel any limiting thoughts on the topic of the divine.

Rabbi Leder says:

> *When people say to me, you know, I'm not a believer, I don't believe in God, I just say, well, what do you believe in? And they always, always, without exception, go on to articulate a very deeply spiritual concept. They'll say something like nature, or humanity, or love, which are the things that I mean when I say God... And so I, I just tell people, use whatever word you want. I don't care. Do you think you made the sun rise this morning? No, we all know there's something at work greater than us and whatever you want to call it is fine with me. We're all describing the same mystery. And I'm okay with that because the word [God] has in a way been so monopolized that it's verboten for most of us.*[37]

For our quest to be successful, we must accept a higher power as a given for two reasons. First, it gives us a sense of humility, reminding us of our limitations and allowing us to receive help from others. Second, it allows us to acknowledge factors beyond our control, such as our inherited genetics and our family of origin, so we can focus on the things that will actually move the needle for us.[v]

FINDING JOY IS THE TRUE NORTH

After Hoffman, despite the boost from my newfound spirituality, I was in a unique position in my life where I lacked a sense of purpose. I had sold my business, so I was flush with cash, time, and made-up prestige. My identity was still tied to my role as a CEO, and without the title I felt rudderless.

I found myself in constant pursuit of desire. Instead of finding comfort in my life's lull, I relied on quick hits of pleasure from shopping, drugs, love, and sex.[vi] Chasing pleasure in this manner, I soon learned, only leads to chronic

---

v   To be clear, I'm not conflating belief in the concept of God or some higher power with religion. The concepts of religion and belief in a higher power are intertwined but distinct. Religion is an organized system built upon specific dogmatic beliefs, whereas believing in a higher power is a broader and more personal conviction that can exist with or without a particular religion.

vi   I wish I would have discovered the 12-Step recovery program sooner than I did. If you're struggling with these or any other addictions or compulsions from food to work to everything in between, there's literally no reason to not check out a meeting. It's free, anonymous, and takes place daily either in-person or online.

dissatisfaction because neither the physical body nor the ego can ever truly be satisfied.[38]

After several shameful experiences, burned bridges, squandered time, and wasted money, I resolved to stop acting in a counterproductive manner. I began to study happiness so I could start acting like an adult.

One of the books I read was *The Happiness Hypothesis* by prominent social psychologist Jonathan Haidt. He determined that happiness doesn't stem from superficiality nor enlightenment. It stems from "between" the two ends of this spectrum. It comes from both paths working in concert. According to Haidt, "You have to get the conditions right and then wait."[39]

But what were these conditions?

Sonja Lyubomirsky, a positive psychology researcher, conducted research revealing that up to 40 percent of our happiness is derived from intentional activities.

This important data point prompted a more pointed question: *In what ways can I optimize my intentional activities to maximize happiness?*

That's when it hit me: belonging. By discovering and optimizing the intentional activities in my life through the lens of belonging, I would find greater fulfillment and experience more joy. Unlike the fleeting highs of pleasure and the fluctuating— often dependent—nature of happiness, joy is lasting and deep. Happiness is like a sparkler, and joy is like the sun.

Joy is the True North of the journey, and it will emerge when we unearth our sense of belonging.

Joy Is the True North

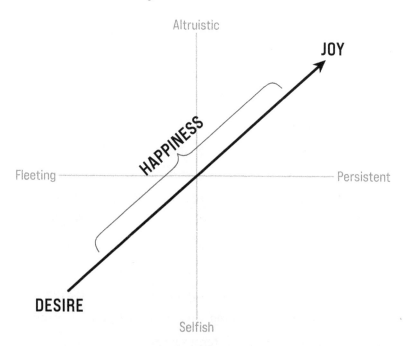

NO WINNERS OR LOSERS IN THE CORTICAL LOTTERY

Divine rights, bloodlines, and aristocracy were the cornerstones of the social hierarchy leading up to the seventeenth and eighteenth centuries. To undermine the assertions of the elite class of the time, Enlightenment philosopher John Locke popularized the old concept of *tabula rasa*, or "the blank slate." This doctrine asserts that humans are born devoid of

> **Joy is the True North of the journey, and it will emerge when we unearth our sense of belonging.**

mental content. This was an important milestone in his argument for the inalienable, "natural" rights of man. In suggesting that humans are blank slates, he implied that our experiences are what shape many of our personality traits.

Modern science has left little doubt that the doctrine of the blank slate is false. We now know that genetics make up 40–50 percent of our personality traits, including how our happiness is derived.[40] This doesn't necessarily imply that some people are born to rule, but it does suggest that a lot has already been decided for you through your *genetic set point*, or the baseline level for certain traits that you inherited from your parents. Haidt charmingly refers to this as the *cortical lottery*.

Lyubomirsky concurs with these assertions, saying that genetics decide up to 50 percent of our overall happiness.[41]

TRACEROUTING JOY

If up to 50 percent is spoken for, where does the rest of our happiness come from?

The other 50 percent is made up of the intentional activities you participate in (40 percent) and the environmental factors around you (10 percent). In other words, as much as 50 percent of our happiness (or joy for all intents and purposes) is 100 percent controllable. It is in these slices of the pie where we will be spending most of our time throughout The Quest.

What Determines Happiness?[vii]

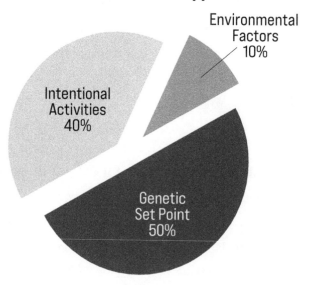

Three primary factors influencing the chronic happiness level

To better understand the relationship among these three components—genetic set point, intentional activities, and environmental factors—I like to use the Serenity Prayer. Commonly found in Alcoholics Anonymous meetings, the prayer requests acceptance, courage, and wisdom from a higher power to help individuals cope during times of need.

---

vii   These percentages don't mean that for each person, exactly 50 percent of their happiness comes from genetics, 10 percent from life circumstances, and 40 percent from intentional activities. Instead, they mean that when you look at the whole population, these factors explain the variation in happiness levels between them. In other words, if you were to look at why one person is happier than another, about 50 percent of that difference might be due to genetic differences, 10 percent to differences in their life circumstances, and 40 percent to differences in their intentional activities.

[God], grant me the serenity
to accept the things I cannot change,
the courage to change the things I can,
and the wisdom to know the difference.

Putting the word *God* aside for one moment, let's focus on the three remaining lines. The second line is a plea for the emotional intelligence to accept where we placed in the cortical lottery. We then appeal for strength to change anything that doesn't serve us. The final line is a hope for the ability to accept the realities of life as they are—to work *around* them instead of *against* them.

Now, let's return to the first line.

EXERCISE   *Complete this digitally at belongingquest.com/exercises*

YOUR SPIRITUAL ORIENTATION

When it comes to the prayer's opening line, you can choose whichever word resonates with your own spiritual beliefs (e.g., Creator, Light, Source, Universe, etc.) as a substitute for "God." Here is a handy guide to help you figure this out if you need some help.

Your Spiritual Orientation

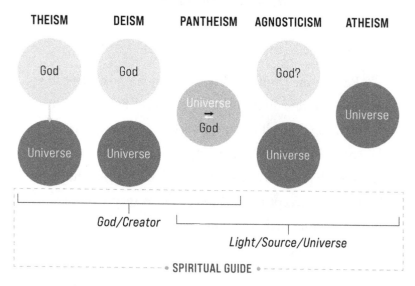

Theism includes various beliefs, but, fundamentally, it asserts the existence of a personal, interactive deity or deities who take interest in and sometimes intervene in human matters.

Deism suggests that a divine creator, often referred to as the "First Cause" or "Prime Mover," started the universe and established its natural laws. Advocates of this belief system firmly assert that the creator does not intervene in human affairs or the ongoing operations of the world.

Pantheism perceives the divine as being synonymous with the universe in its entirety, encompassing every element of nature and existence and attributing divinity to each.

Agnosticism maintains that we cannot be certain about matters of the divine or that we lack the knowledge to confirm or reject such beliefs.

Atheism is the denial of belief in any gods or deities, typically relying solely on empirical evidence, science, and rationality.

If you're an atheist, as I once was, try considering a different perspective, even just for this exercise. What other viewpoints might you explore? How do they make you feel? In my opinion, agnosticism represents a more elevated consciousness than atheism; instead of outright denying the existence of a higher power, agnosticism involves questioning and being receptive to unknown possibilities.

PURSUING THE CLIMB

In The Quest, I'll be emphasizing the significance of consistently striving to foster a sense of belonging. This ongoing pursuit is an integral aspect of the abstract concept often referred to as *the work* or *the process.* For our purposes, it's *the climb.* This climb drives us to become better people as we navigate whatever lies ahead.

Focusing on the climb as life unfolds gives us a greater purpose than simply allowing life to happen to us. It moves us from passive attendees to active participants. Embracing it instead of shunning it, with all its shades of tragedy and humor, makes our stay much more enjoyable.

The psychiatrist Phil Stutz, who rose to prominence in part thanks to Jonah Hill's documentary *Stutz,* says that the work is what life is all about: "[It] is what you're here to do. It's what you were born to do. [It] is the one thing that gives your life meaning. It's the one thing that makes all the other things worth doing."[42]

When I recounted the visuals I saw during my psilocybin journey to my guide, she told me of *Kintsugi*—the Japanese art of repairing broken pottery. By using natural lacquer mixed with gold, silver, or platinum, the broken pieces are repaired and celebrated instead of being hidden in shame. The breakage is celebrated through the object's inherent continuity. Like the lacquer used in *Kintsugi*, our spiritual beliefs act as a golden filler that can mend us when we feel broken.

As I heard this analogy, it suddenly hit me: *broken is okay.*

Much like our broken—and repaired—parts, some aspects that influence our happiness cannot be changed. There are, however, plenty of things *within* our control that drive our happiness; let's focus on them during our climb.

> There are, however, plenty of things *within* our control that drive our happiness; let's focus on them during our climb.

CHAPTER 5

ORIENTING TO THE TERRAIN

*"Many paths lead from the foot of the mountain, but
at the peak we all gaze at the single bright moon."*
—IKKYU

As I entered my forties, I moved to my new home state of
Idaho with great enthusiasm and a little too much determination. Eager to reinvent myself after closing my last entrepreneurial chapter, I made a conscious effort to engage with my
new environment in various ways.

The first step was posting on LinkedIn about my plans to
relocate. Within a few days, I had a list of friends-of-friends to
reach out to for coffee. This marked the beginning of dozens
of coffee meetings during my first few months in town.

I joined a local coworking space to immerse myself in the
city's ecosystem. Additionally, I became a member of various
affinity groups, including the local chapter of the Entrepre-
neurs' Organization and the local Chamber of Commerce. I

even joined a supper club where Idaho's old guard, including the governor, gathered at lunchtime for a game of Gin Rummy.

Given that Idaho is nearly 70 percent wilderness, I felt compelled to experience the outdoors, so I bought a camper. Towing it with my Tesla highlighted just how unprepared I was for this new lifestyle.

I pursued hobbies that had previously intimidated me, such as snowboarding, martial arts, and running, challenging myself to overcome my physical insecurities and body dysmorphia. I also joined a boutique gym to make my workouts more social. To give back, I organized a couple of learning sessions for Boise's Entrepreneur Week, served as its cohost, and joined its organizing committee.

I joined an angel investor group and invested in several local start-ups. I also financially backed a commercial cleaning company started by an ambitious Serbian entrepreneur named Nikola. Today, four years after we started it, Executive Cleaning of Idaho is generating $1 million in annual revenue.

To bridge the knowledge gap about my new home and catch up with the locals, I bought audiobooks and read up on the state's history. I even joined a local synagogue and eventually started a nonprofit to fight antisemitism.

Finally, and perhaps most proudly, I started a men's community called Fellas and Firepits, which today has twenty-five members. We host monthly in-person gatherings at different members' homes and have an online discussion group as well. We have strict attendance rules—you can't miss more than one meeting per quarter—and we require attendees to stay for the entire duration of an event.

I know it sounds like I did a ton—and I did. But remember, I didn't have any other commitments during this period of my life. Additionally, many of these activities faded. Ninety percent of them didn't last. In fact, I was either actively or passively rejected from most of these pursuits. While each rejection stung and every departure brought a bit of shame, I now realize it was the forcing function I needed to help me figure out where I belonged. Rejection is much better than the alternative of contorting myself to fit in.

Little did I know that through all of this madness, I was actually following a tried-and-true process of finding belonging.

STORAGE FOR OUR SENSE OF BELONGING

The **belonging fuel tank** is a container that holds all the "fuels," or intentional activities, we participate in that help us fill our sense of belonging. Each fuel represents a unique strategy to engage in, ranging from pursuing hobbies to spending time in nature—and everything in between. The tank is a handy visual representation of how much or how little our belonging needs are being met.

I modeled the belonging fuel tank after the social fuel

> The tank is a handy visual representation of how much or how little our belonging needs are being met.

tank developed by psychologist Elaine Paravati and colleagues.[43] I modified its name since, as we will soon discover,
not all belonging activities involve actual socializing.

Each person has their own unique combination of fuels,
and the number of fuels depends on the person's archetype.
One study revealed that two-thirds of people had a range of
two to seventeen activities in their tank, with an average of
almost eight.[44]

The Belonging Tank

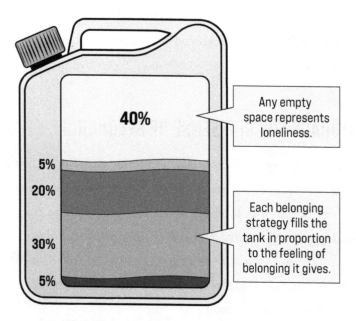

Any empty space represents loneliness.

40%

5%
20%

Each belonging strategy fills the tank in proportion to the feeling of belonging it gives.

30%

5%

THE SIX BELONGING FUELS

Beginning with Maslow in the 1940s through the first decade
of the twenty-first century, psychologists only focused on

how belonging relates to close relationships.[45] Starting in the 2010s, scholars observed new ways we fulfill our belonging needs, which go beyond traditionally social activities.

The belonging fuel tank encompasses both eras of belonging. *Traditional fuels* comprise conventional means of connection, such as spending time with a spouse or friends. *Nontraditional fuels* include symbolic attachments and contemplative practices.

According to research, traditional fuels are highly valued by a large portion of the population. In one study, participants were asked what fuels they "filled" their tanks with. Eighty-five percent of people named time spent with family and close friends, while 50 percent named time spent with a romantic partner.

The same study revealed nontraditional paths as equally vital. Seventy-five percent of people used music as a means of connection, while over half used TV to fill their belonging fuel tanks.[46] This mix reflects the complexity of human social needs and the innovative ways in which we seek to satisfy them in our contemporary world.[47]

Now that we have a high-level understanding of the two major fuel categories, I'd like to introduce you to the six major fuels that help people find belonging. After carefully analyzing the research and adding my own interpretations, I have compiled this list. I have further refined this list to include **subfuels**, secondary paths that we can leverage within each primary fuel category. This model isn't flawless, but my intention is to make it accessible to everyone while covering a wide range of belonging strategies.

The fuels are interpersonal relationships, collective experiences, casual encounters, symbolic bonds, esteem-building, and contemplative practices. Each of them has a handful of subfuels, making the potential permutations to fill our belonging fuel tanks virtually endless!

Think of these fuels as different paths on our journey up the mountain. Some are well-maintained and easy to traverse, while others are rugged and more challenging. As we explore all the available belonging fuels, I invite you to keep an open mind. Just as a path might offer a shortcut to the summit or lead you to a new vantage point, different fuels will resonate with you to varying degrees. Some may align perfectly with your belonging needs, while others may not.

The Six Belonging Fuels

 Interpersonal Relationships: Relationships marked by deep bonds and secure attachment.

 Collective Experiences: Membership, participation, or affiliation in a collective.

 Casual Encounters: Social interactions that give us connection but lack depth.

 Symbolic Bonds: Connections to someone else without their presence.

 Esteem-Building: Status-seeking activities for approval and/or praise.

 Contemplative Practices: Focusing on finding connectedness within, with a higher power, or with the universe.

BEWARE OF THE FALSE SUMMITS

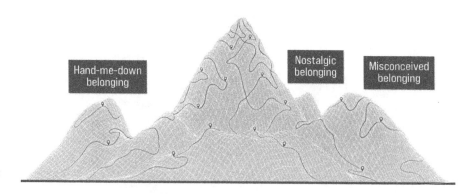

As with any difficult endeavor, there are dead ends that appear promising but ultimately lead nowhere, and our quest is no different. The first such false summit is *hand-me-down belonging*.

As children, our direction in life is largely shaped by our parents, teachers, or key figures during our upbringing. They influence our living situation, religion, sports, schools, hobbies, and sometimes even our career choices. However, as we grow older and more independent, we come to understand that we have more control over our sense of belonging than we initially thought. We're no longer bound by our parents' preferences.

> As with any difficult endeavor, there are dead ends that appear promising but ultimately lead nowhere, and our quest is no different.

A second false summit is *nostalgic belonging*. This is when we hold on to emotional connections that are fading. We do this because we are sentimental or optimistic by nature. You might still be hanging out with your college friend group even if the group is devoid of intimacy. Or you may still be participating in an affinity group that shares the same passion, but everyone in it is unkind. You hold on to the hope that the next iteration of community guidelines will change things for the better.

Misconceived belonging forms our third false summit. It often arises from not fully understanding our belonging needs or the true sources of our sense of belonging. Take the workplace, for example. Many people believe their workplace provides them with a sense of belonging, but it's more nuanced than that. It's the social aspects of our job—the friendships, potential romantic partners, casual encounters, crowd participation, and group membership—that makes up this feeling of belonging.

EXERCISE *Complete this digitally at belongingquest.com/exercises*

ENTRY BELONGING FUEL TANK

Before we learn about the belonging fuels that we have at our disposal in greater detail, let's create the first version of your very own belonging fuel tank.

1. List all the activities that give you a sense of belonging. Don't overthink them—if an activity comes to you, jot it down. To ensure its relevance to your present life, make sure you have engaged in that activity within the last year or so. Feel free to collect extra credit by avoiding false summits. For reference purposes, here's a list of the activities your tank might contain:

Watching films	Eating favorite foods	Being involved in special interest groups
Following celebrities or influencers online	Listening to music	Watching television shows or movies
Working with colleagues or classmates	Exercises in group settings	Attending large group events
Chatting with acquaintances	Practicing meditation	Playing video games
Reading books	Interacting in online forums, chat rooms, or communities	Looking at nostalgic photos or mementos
Meeting acquaintances	Hanging out in coffee shops	Interacting with family members
Greeting neighbors	Celebrating cultural or religious events	Being part of a large crowd at an event
Spending time with close friends	Managing your social media profile	Engaging in prayer
Taking part in movements or causes	Following celebrities	Caring for pets
Spending time with your spouse or partner	Partaking in a hobby	Volunteering for a cause

2. Distribute up to but no more than one hundred points among the activities on your list. Assign points to each activity based on how much it contributes to your sense of belonging, giving more points to the activities that you care about the most.

3. Convert the points to percentages. Since you started with one hundred points, each point will equal 1 percent. Add up the percentages to see how full your tank is. What's your total?

No.	Activity	Percentage
1		
2		
3		
4		
5		
6		
7		
8		
9		
10		
11		

Consider the difference between the sum of your fuels and a full tank (100 percent) as "loneliness," but not in a negative way. In fact, it's an opportunity to add more belonging to your life. There will be plenty of mechanisms to address this gap throughout our quest.

Again, this is only version one. You have two more to go through The Quest, so it does not have to be perfect. This instance captures a snapshot of how you've found belonging throughout your life up to this point. This was an unintentional way of belonging, shaped mostly by your intuition. It was a passive experience of feeling connected to others without deliberate effort. As we progress toward the summit, we will become more intentional about filling our fuel tank.

> **This was an unintentional way of belonging, shaped mostly by your intuition.**

CHAPTER 6

GEARING UP FOR THE ASCENT

"The cave you fear to enter holds the treasure that you seek."
—JOSEPH CAMPBELL

My best friend Matt's lack of engagement with our friend group, solitary behavioral patterns, and intense focus on his personal hobbies frustrated me for years. After all, we were more similar than not. Both of us were adopted children, we grew up with no siblings in the home, and we were raised mostly by a single mother. I couldn't figure out why he wasn't doing exactly what I was doing to find belonging.

This was a source of not-so-silent resentment for years. I would often get mad at him for not being an active participant in our friend group's text thread and for not reading its hundreds of daily messages. I couldn't understand why he didn't take the time to get to know the newer additions to the group like he knew me. The story I told myself was that he was not valuing our social crew and thus our friendship. And I wasn't afraid to yell at him for this injustice from time to time.

One of the realizations that came to me as I was writing this book is that I was thinking of belonging the wrong way. I was approaching it as a one-size-fits-all framework. If I could just map out how to find belonging for myself, I could help everyone else find it too. I eventually came to my senses: a reductionist attitude wouldn't serve me well in this endeavor.

Whether it's me, Matt, or you, each of us finds belonging in different ways. While I thrive in social settings and enjoy group activities, Matt finds solace in his solitary interests, annual camping trips, and one-on-one deep dives with close friends. This basic yet profound realization was a moment of clarity for me.

A CUSTOMIZED BELONGING PROFILE

The **belonging archetype** is a fingerprint of how each of us finds belonging. It's a composite of two independent psychological constructs: *attachment style* and *need to belong scale*, or *NTBS*. These determinants were formed by our genetic set point and our upbringing until we were twelve years old. By this age, psychologists agree, most people have typically formed the essential psychological and social building blocks that will shape the rest of their lives.

> The belonging archetype is a fingerprint of how each of us finds belonging.

To make our quest personal yet manageable, I've crafted four unique archetypes. To make it accessible and memorable,

I used well-known animals with distinct personality traits. We will leverage these archetypes to choose the unique strategies that work best for you.

Attachment style refers to the consistent patterns of thoughts, feelings, and behaviors people exhibit in relationships. NTBS measures a person's desire for acceptance and reflects their intrinsic need to be part of a social network. Together, these constructs provide a comprehensive understanding of how you form relationships and your inherent need for social connection. Although there are many psychological tools available for the purposes of studying how we feel connected, I have discovered that these two are most effective for our purposes.

EVERY STYLE IS A MATCH

Attachment theory, pioneered by psychologist John Bowlby, helps explain how humans form emotional bonds, connect with others, and seek comfort when experiencing duress. There are four main attachment styles.

Knowing our attachment style can be a useful self-awareness tool for understanding and improving how we show up in social settings, especially when it comes to interpersonal relationships. Unlike in fashion, your attachment style always looks good and is never out of season. Here are the four main attachment styles:

- **Secure Attachment.** Adults who possess a secure attachment style experience relationships that are healthy, trusting, and enduring. When in a romantic partnership, there is a sense of comfort in communicating emotions and acknowledging the other partner's needs.

- **Dismissive-Avoidant Attachment.** Adults who possess this attachment style often have trouble with intimacy and may push their partner away when things get too serious or emotional. They may downplay the significance of close connections and occasionally come across as apathetic.

- **Anxious-Preoccupied Attachment.** Adults who possess this attachment style may be perceived as dependent or overly reliant in their relationships, often seeking frequent reassurance. Their relationship status is a constant concern for them, and any indications of rejection can easily hurt them.

- **Fearful-Avoidant Attachment.** Adults who possess this attachment style often experience mixed emotions regarding close interpersonal connections. This fear frequently causes them to withdraw, resulting in a pattern of avoidance even if they desire to be close. They experience difficulties in placing trust in others, due to their fear of rejection or abandonment, resulting in a fluctuation between intimacy and distance within their relationships.

Secure attachment is the healthiest of the four styles because it denotes a safe space for individuals, allowing them to explore the world with the confidence that their partner or caregiver will comfort them and provide for them.

The remaining styles are considered insecure because they may lead to patterns of behavior or emotional responses that hinder the development of healthy, stable, and trusting relationships.

EXERCISE *Complete this digitally at belongingquest.com/exercises*

YOUR ATTACHMENT STYLE

To simplify matters, we will divide attachment styles into two categories: **secure** and **insecure.**

1. Carefully read the four statements below. Each one portrays a distinct emotional experience people may have in their relationships with partners or caregivers.

2. Rate each statement from zero to five, with zero meaning it does not describe you at all, and five meaning it describes you exceptionally well.

   Statement 1 | I am comfortable without close emotional relationships. I really don't want to rely on anyone or have anyone rely on me because I value my independence and self-sufficiency.

   | 0 | 1 | 2 | 3 | 4 | 5 |

Statement 2 | I've noticed that others are not as open to getting as close as I would prefer. I'm always paranoid that my partner doesn't really love me or won't want to stick around. All I want is to be completely "one" with another person, but sometimes it freaks them out.

0   1   2   3   4   5

Statement 3 | Building close bonds with others comes naturally to me, and I feel completely at ease relying on them and being relied upon in return. The thought of being abandoned or of someone getting too close to me rarely crosses my mind.

0   1   2   3   4   5

Statement 4 | I don't like getting too close to people. I really want to connect with others, but it's tough for me to trust or count on them. I'm worried I'll get hurt if I get too close to people.

0   1   2   3   4   5

3. The statement that scores the highest points reveals your attachment style. This is the style that accurately depicts your approach to close relationships.

If Statement 3 received your highest rating, then you have a predominant attachment style of secure. If Statement 1, Statement 2, or Statement 4 received your highest rating, your primary attachment style is insecure. Make a note of whether you have a secure or insecure attachment style, as we will use this information to determine your belonging archetype later in this chapter.

For our purposes, I created this exceptionally simplified attachment style quiz. If you want a more reliable albeit slightly longer test (twelve questions), search the web for "Experience in Close Relationship Scale" or "ECR-S."

REMEDIES TO INSECURE ATTACHMENT

My childhood traumas of neglect and caregiver insecurity have made it hard for me to form secure attachments—I still have work to do. If you have a low score on Statement 3 (secure attachment), it's likely because of similar circumstances in your early life that were out of your control. While it is not your fault, it is your responsibility to address any insecure attachment if you desire a better life, psychological safety, and a healthy sense of belonging.

Attachment style is generally considered a stable aspect of our personality, but research indicates that it can change with considerable effort. Here are three remedies adapted from Haidt's *The Happiness Hypothesis* to invest in

> While it is not your fault, it is your responsibility to address any insecure attachment if you desire a better life, psychological safety, and a healthy sense of belonging.

forming a more secure attachment style. Please note that the remedies below are based solely on my experience.

Note: The information provided here is based on personal experiences and should not be considered professional psychological advice. Individual experiences vary greatly, and it's important to consult with a licensed professional for personalized guidance, support, and treatment.

Remedy #1 | Psychotherapy

Psychotherapy is a broad term that encompasses the different treatments available for mental health conditions, including anxiety, trauma, post-traumatic stress disorder (PTSD), stress disorders, and depression. It involves working with a licensed mental health professional to identify and address negative thoughts, feelings, and behaviors. Only after several years of seeing a traditional "talk therapy" therapist did I realize that there are many other therapeutic modalities available. I wish I had discovered this sooner.

Addressing and modifying patterns behind attachment issues can help reshape your attachment style. For me, the most effective modality was internal family systems, or IFS, also known as "parts work." This approach taught me that, like everyone, I have an army of protectors that come to my aid with the best intentions when I am in pain or face a perceived threat. Unfortunately, these protectors don't always act appropriately. In my case, they responded with unexplainable anger and even rage. Understanding their origins and recognizing that they are just *parts of me*, not my whole self, helped me grow.

Another effective technique is eye movement desensitization and reprocessing, or EMDR, which has shown great promise in helping individuals with trauma-related issues. EMDR uses guided eye movements to enable the reprocessing of traumatic memories. Think of it like paying a visit to yourself when you were child to impart wisdom from your present-day adult self to them. A related and more accessible form of therapy involves bilateral stimulation. Companies like Dharma Dr. are making it easier to access such tools at home.[viii] According to founder Brad Mosell, when combined with traditional therapy, EMDR and similar treatments can enhance therapy's effectiveness by aiding in emotional processing and speeding up the healing of traumatic memories.

Cognitive therapy offers tools and strategies that directly address the root causes of attachment issues. This allows individuals to better interpret and respond to their triggers in more mature ways and thus have healthier relationships with the people they care most about. Remember, just because one psychotherapeutic technique may not have worked for you, it does not mean others will have the same fate.

Remedy #2 | Pharmacotherapy

Medications like selective serotonin reuptake inhibitors (SSRIs) and therapeutic sessions with psychedelics can help stabilize mood and reduce chronic anxiety caused by insecure attachment. Furthermore, they have the potential to help indi-

---

viii   I'm an angel investor in this company.

viduals confront and possibly redefine past traumas, leading to the development of healthier relationship patterns.

Lexapro, a widely prescribed SSRI for anxiety management, has made a significant positive impact on my life with minimal side effects. My therapist prescribed it when I began experiencing heart palpitations, panic attacks, and irritable bowel syndrome (IBS) resulting from persistent rumination or incessant overthinking. By providing a new, less anxious baseline, Lexapro has made me less reactive in my relationships, positively contributing to a more secure attachment style.

A growing number of companies are exploring the use of various psychedelics, aside from psilocybin, to assist individuals in their healing process. Focalpoint Partners, an early-stage venture capital fund run by Brom Rector, has witnessed the alternative medicine industry firsthand.[ix] Brom told me about a few of their most exciting companies. Their investments include Lykos Therapeutics, which is working on FDA approval for the drug MDMA; TARA Mind, offering ketamine therapy as an employee benefit; and Beond, which is providing medically supervised ibogaine therapy in Mexico.

Like psychotherapy, not all drugs work for all people. In fact, only four out of ten people treated with antidepressants improve with the first one they try.[48] Adding to the complexity of this issue, certain medications will offer only a partial relief from what ails you, so you may need to use trial and error in order to figure out what works best for you.

---

ix   I'm a limited partner in this fund.

Remedy #3 | Meditation

Meditation, when practiced regularly, can positively alter brain regions involved in stress response, emotional regulation, self-awareness, compassion, and cognitive processing.[49] In other words, by promoting a calm and centered mind, meditation can improve our brain's functionality. Such improvements can usher in a more secure attachment style.

Not so ironically, meditation is also one of our belonging fuels, so using this remedy is a win-win. We will cover it in much more detail at high camp.

EXERCISE   *Complete this digitally at belongingquest.com/exercises*

WHAT REMEDIES WILL YOU TRY?

If like me you have struggled with an insecure attachment style, what's your plan to remedy it? What commitments can you make to yourself right now to improve this critical component of your emotional well-being?

THE BELONG-O-METER

The purpose of the NTBS is to measure an individual's sense of belongingness, specifically their tendency to seek acceptance and inclusion in social circles. This scale operates on the premise that humans possess an intrinsic need for belonging, which deeply influences their mental processes, behaviors, and emotional experiences.[50] Think of it like your belonging energy level—the greater the score, the greater your need to feel belonging.

- **High NTBS**: Individuals with high scores on the NTBS demonstrate a keen awareness of how they are perceived by others and have a strong inclination to take part in social activities to feel accepted. They feel anxious or sad when they think they're being rejected, closely watching how people respond. They also invest considerable effort in actively taking part in social circles and nurturing their relationships, as these factors are vital to their sense of self.

- **Low NTBS**: Individuals with low NTBS scores prioritize their independence and remain unaffected by social pressure. They are typically unconcerned with others' perceptions in social settings and maintain emotional stability regardless of social cues. They value personal fulfillment over seeking approval, resulting in deeper connections with fewer people.

EXERCISE *Complete this digitally at belongingquest.com/exercises*

YOUR NEED TO BELONG[51]

Let's calculate your NTBS score.

1. For each of the ten statements below, use a one to five scale to indicate whether you agree or disagree, where one is Strongly Disagree, and five is Strongly Agree:

- If people don't accept me, it really bothers me

  1   2   3   4   5

- I avoid doing things that will make people dislike me

  1   2   3   4   5

- Sometimes I wonder if other people care about me

  1   2   3   4   5

- I need people I can rely on in tough times

  1   2   3   4   5

- I want others to accept me

  1   2   3   4   5

- I dislike being alone

  1   2   3   4   5

- I hate being away from my friends for too long

  1   2   3   4   5

- I have a strong need for belonging

  1   2   3   4   5

- Being excluded from social events really bothers me

1   2   3   4   5

- I'm easily hurt if I sense others don't accept me

1   2   3   4   5

2. Calculate the average of the statements to get your NTBS score.

A score higher than 2.5 indicates a higher need to belong, while a score lower than 2.5 indicates a lower need to belong. By referring to this chart, you can determine how your result compares to the general population. The bell curve tells us that the data is normally distributed.

The General Population's Need to Belong Score

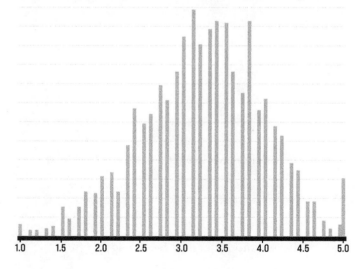

CHANGES TO THE NTBS

Although your NTBS score is often treated as a stable measure, it is important to recognize that it can change over time due to several factors. Major life changes, such as starting school, beginning a new job, or starting a family, can significantly influence our need to belong. These introductions of new environments or relationships can cause our NTBS score to fluctuate.

As we grow older, our social networks typically shrink in size but increase in emotional quality. This

Major life changes, such as starting school, beginning a new job, or starting a family, can significantly influence our need to belong.

has a downstream impact on how we value and prioritize social connections and thus impacts our NTBS score. Additionally, as our personalities evolve, our approach to belonging may change as well. For instance, becoming more extroverted or introverted, experiencing changes in self-esteem, or undergoing personal growth can all move our NTBS score up or down.

EXERCISE *Complete this digitally at belongingquest.com/exercises*

YOUR ARCHETYPE

Now that you know the two determinants that make up your belonging archetype, you can properly identify which of the four profiles is your match.

1. Determine whether you fall into the right or left quadrants (x-axis) based on your attachment style. The right quadrant is secure attachment, and the left quadrant is insecure attachment.

2. Based on your NTBS score, place yourself in the vertical quadrant (y-axis). The top quadrant is a score greater than or equal to 2.5 and the bottom quadrant is a score less than 2.5.

3. I recognize there's a chance you are not right in a single quadrant, and that's okay. Having a blended profile means that you are influenced by both a primary and secondary archetype. With a blended profile, you can discover an even greater range of belonging avenues, which I'll present in this book.

HIGH NEED TO BELONG

ANXIOUS
BELONGING

EAGER
BELONGING

INSECURE ATTACHMENT — SECURE ATTACHMENT

RELUCTANT
BELONGING

INDEPENDENT
BELONGING

LOW NEED TO BELONG

Understanding your archetype will help us customize how you go about finding belonging throughout The Quest. It will assist you in navigating social relationships more effectively and finding environments where you feel most included and valued.

THE STARTING LINEUP

The Chimpanzee (Eager Belonging)

High NTBS and Secure Attachment

Belonging comes easily to chimpanzees because they thrive in social settings. Their positive emotions fuel effortless interactions, forming the foundation of strong bonds within their complex communities. This deep need to belong translates to heightened happiness when included and profound distress when excluded.

Their exceptional social skills manifest in cooperation, problem-solving as a group, and a strong sense of empathy. These down-to-earth creatures rely heavily on their social network, showcasing an attachment style that prioritizes secure bonds.

Their intense desire for connection, however, can be a double-edged sword. Chimps may disregard personal boundaries or become overly invested in maintaining social standing.

The Meerkat (Anxious Belonging)

High NTBS and Insecure Attachment

Unlike chimps who relish social connection, belonging can be a struggle for meerkats. They crave companionship, evidenced by their positive emotions around others and the distress of rejection. However, their insecure attachment style often backfires. This can lead to behaviors like anxiety and negativity that might unintentionally distance them from others, hindering their desire for strong bonds.

Their constant communication and alertness within the group are a double-edged sword. While cooperation thrives, so does a pervasive sense of caution.

Meerkats excel at social vigilance, a likely consequence of past trauma. They yearn for connection and offer strong support within their circles. However, their insecurities make them prone to overreacting to slights and overly reliant on reassurance.

The Snow Leopard (Reluctant Belonging)

Low NTBS and Insecure Attachment

Snow leopards have a mixed and unenthusiastic attitude toward belonging. Their solitary nature and cautious attachment style lead them to prefer independence over constant companionship. This can sometimes result in behaviors that might unintentionally create distance with others or drive them away.

These majestic cats embody the concept of comfortable solitude. Their interactions with others are specific and often limited to their romantic partner. This preference for limited social engagement aligns with those who value their independence and a more reserved social life.

Snow leopards excel at self-reliance and can form deep connections when they choose to. They face challenges with opening up and trusting others. They often choose to be alone, which can lead to social isolation.

The Wolf (Independent Belonging)

Low NTBS and Secure Attachment

Unlike the rest of our creatures, wolves find a comfortable balance between being social and being independent. In a way, they have the easiest time finding belonging because of their resilience and adaptability.

Their secure attachment style fosters healthy relationships within their pack, and their low need to belong allows them to thrive without constant social validation. This adaptability allows them to navigate social situations with ease, expressing positive emotions and behaviors that strengthen their connections.

These adaptable canines excel at balancing social interaction with solitude. They demonstrate resilience in overcoming challenges, and they maintain healthy boundaries. Their self-sufficiency, sometimes perceived as aloofness, might initially hinder connection attempts.

Wolves exemplify a harmonious approach to relationships. They forge strong bonds within their pack, yet their self-reliant spirit allows them to survive even if they are left to fend for themselves. This adaptability reflects individuals comfortable in their own skin, capable of forming deep connections while cherishing their independence.

FROM ANXIOUS MEERKAT TO EAGER CHIMP

While my NTBS score won't change anytime soon due to my innate need for social connection, I have been working on addressing my insecure attachment style for years, slowly evolving from an anxious meerkat to an eager chimp. Reflecting on the jealousy and anxiety I displayed in previous relationships, I now view that behavior with a healthy dose of appropriate guilt.

The first step I took to address my traumas was to understand the nature of my adoption abandonment. For years, I felt an insatiable urge to seek out my biological family. Initially, my reason seemed straightforward and selfless—I wanted to find my birth mom and express gratitude for the difficult decision she made in giving me up for adoption. However, I soon realized that my actions were driven by more than just gratitude.

The true impetus for my search was a desire to confront and heal the abandonment I faced as a child. Meeting my biological mother allowed me to see what my life could have been like if I hadn't been adopted. This alternate reality was not pretty; I would have been worse off than I had been as an adoptee. This encounter fostered a deeper appreciation for my adoption, despite its pain and complexity. It marked the beginning of my healing process.

More recently, I attended a weeklong intensive trauma treatment at Psychological Counseling Services, or PCS. This seventy-hour therapy program has been the most impactful healing experience I have ever had. Discussing all my takeaways would fill a book on its own, but the most significant learning was that the abandonment I had faced had given me a lot of sadness. Up until that week, I had never given my sadness the understanding nor the permission to come out. When it finally did, I felt so much emotional and physical relief.

Regardless of your archetype or the kind of pain you've endured, the fact is that you are still here, on this quest, climbing. The best way to move toward joy in your life is to fill your belonging needs. Up next is high camp, where we will learn about all the belonging opportunities that await us.

STAGE III
HIGH CAMP

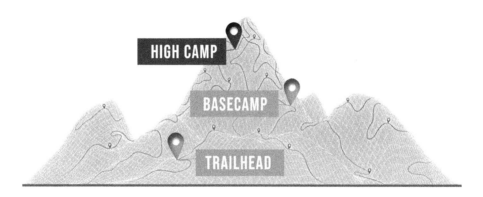

HIGH CAMP

BASECAMP

TRAILHEAD

CHAPTER 7

REDISCOVERING TRADITIONAL BELONGING PATHS

"The good life is built with good relationships."
—ROBERT J. WALDINGER

There was a period in my life when my unwavering dedication to the company I founded overshadowed everything else, including my search for love. During this era, seriously dating someone just wasn't a priority. My business was what I thought about when I went to bed and when I woke up. It's all I talked about. It was so intertwined with my identity that I got a tattoo of our company logo on my arm.

Today, with the benefit of hindsight, I know I had an unhealthy relationship with my workplace. In fact, it was the only source of fuels for my belonging tank.

I didn't realize this until I left, when all my feelings of belonging evaporated overnight. My self-importance was no longer regularly validated. The invitations to speak at conferences stopped arriving. And my evenings were suddenly free because there were no company get-togethers taking place.

I started actively looking for a partner with whom I could develop a deeper, more meaningful relationship. After a few years of dating and a handful of false starts, my life was forever changed when I met my soulmate and future wife, Jen.

As our relationship grew, things suddenly clicked for me: this is what belonging feels like. Being in a committed relationship with my best friend and romantic partner revealed that belonging is rooted in our most intimate relationships. Part of my conviction in this path comes from the fact that I experienced the other side of it.

Here, in **high camp**, we will spend some time understanding the different fuels and their subfuels. Given that the summit is up ahead, we need to acclimate anyway.

> Being in a committed relationship with my best friend and romantic partner revealed that belonging is rooted in our most intimate relationships.

The interpersonal relationships fuel I previously articulated is one of three traditional belonging paths. The two other fuels we will explore here in high camp are *collective experiences*, such as joining groups and communities, and *casual encounters*, which consists of socializing with acquaintances and strangers alike.

INTERPERSONAL RELATIONSHIPS

The beating hearts of our closest loved ones house our deepest sense of connection and acceptance, making interpersonal relationships a traditional fuel of great strength. This fuel encompasses the strong bonds we develop with romantic partners, close friends, and beloved family members. The hallmarks of these relationships are secure attachment, trust, and mutual understanding. Another differentiating characteristic is their communal nature, which is marked by authentic care for each other's welfare rather than a sense of duty or expectation for reciprocation.

Romantic Partner

The work of evolutionary psychologist Robin Dunbar underscores the importance of having a life partner. Leaning on observations from the societal structure of primates, Dunbar developed a framework for understanding the potential of our social networks—referred to as *Dunbar's Circles*—to showcase the interrelated capacities we have for relationships.

Since the groundbreaking paper was published in 1992, his circles have been met with some criticism questioning their empirical support. Researchers argue that our social network's potential is shaped by various factors—ranging from cultural norms to individual differences—rather than being limited by a fixed cognitive constraint.[52] This research aligns with our work, emphasizing the importance of a personalized approach to managing interpersonal relationships.

It recognizes that different people have different capacities for social connections.

Despite the model's shortcomings, it is still a good frame of reference for how to think of the different relationships in our lives.

Dunbar's Circles

5000 = Known Faces

At the core of Dunbar's Circles is the concept of the *intimates*, the most sacred relationship each of us has, which comprises approximately one and a half individuals: you and a significant other if you have one (hence the 1.5). This pair is your primary secure relationship.

Mates are extremely important to us humans—so much so that Kenrick and his colleagues, the team behind revising Maslow's Hierarchy of Needs to be more aligned with our current understanding of human behavior, ranked "mate retention" and "mate acquisition" as the second and third most important needs in their pyramid.

How to Find a Partner

Finding the right partner isn't easy, but there are several steps you can take.

Get out. If you are currently in a toxic relationship and you can get out safely, do so because it is impeding your progress on The Quest.

Go out. Regularly go out with friends to practice the in-person social skills of meeting new people. Given how poorly everyone is fairing with this skill these days, it will immediately propel your prospects.

Ask for intros. Ask friends you trust for introductions. After all, the people you are most likely to gel with are probably one or two degrees removed from your social circles.

Join interest groups. This is not necessarily to meet like-minded partners but it's to expand your network so that like-minded people can introduce you to their friends.

The apps are trotlines. Join the hottest dating apps to increase the probability of meeting someone, but keep in mind that you're likely to have better success in person because initial face-to-face interactions lead to more positive social bonding outcomes (i.e., intimacy) compared to texting.[53]

Relocate. If you don't have luck where you currently are, I suggest moving to a city with better prospects for finding a compatible partner. Yes, finding a partner is just that important.

Retain a matchmaker. If I were doing it all over again at a later age in life, I'd retain a matchmaker to help me find someone. Meeting the right person will more than pay back your investment.

Mate retention's high rank in the hierarchy is not surprising, given its deep-rooted importance; maintaining a stable partner is a crucial evolutionary aspect of resource sharing and protection. In its truest essence, a romantic relationship builds an invincible emotional bond through dedication, commitment, and support, contributing to our longevity and overall happiness.[54] Its defining characteristic, however, is committed intimacy marked by "all-in" participation, diverse beliefs that are respected, healthy conflict, and respected boundaries.[55]

After meeting your own needs, nothing should be prioritized over your spouse. This includes children—no matter how young; parents—no matter how old; pets—no matter how cute; and so on. In his book *Wired for Love*, psychotherapist Stan Tatkin argues that when partners put each other first, they model a healthy coparenting partnership for their children.

Family

A secure and safe relationship is crucial, as it allows for successful reproduction and, subsequently, mutual parental investment. These are both prerequisites for reaching the top level of the Kenrick pyramid of fundamental human motives: parenting.

The nuclear family plays a vital role in relationships by creating a cycle of love that is unconditional and support that is deep. Healthy families continuously repeat this cycle, making belonging its natural byproduct.

In my interview with Scott Galloway, a professor at New York University's (NYU) Stern School of Business, on the topic of belonging, he emphasized this notion: "Once you have children," he explained, "you can see how important it is to that kid that he or she is loved and supported by you. That is true belonging." This ultimate belonging is when your family feels "intensely loved and supported by you," and you recognize "how much meaning it has for them."[56]

> This ultimate belonging is when your family feels "intensely loved and supported by you," and you recognize "how much meaning it has for them."

Once again, we see how healthy belonging is a continuously reinforced cycle.

Close Friends

As you move past Dunbar's closest circle, you'll discover your *support circle*, which typically consists of no more than five people. This group includes close friends and family members who offer additional layers of emotional and practical support. These individuals are your go-to in difficult moments, your partners in celebrating victories, and the ones you entrust with important aspects of your life.

One perspective I'd like you to consider is that being in this circle requires mutuality. For a relationship to be successful at this level, intimacy needs to be reciprocal. You can make "bids" or invitations into this circle of intimacy, but some people, even those you consider your best friends, may ultimately choose not to meet you there. For most of my life, I often confused my most fun friends with my best friends. Just because we partied together didn't mean our relationship had the depth I needed in my life.

> **For most of my life, I often confused my most fun friends with my best friends.**

In a world where the latest pop culture advice often advocates for "firing" people who no longer align with your journey, I subscribe to the author Olga Khazan's approach: seek new friends while letting stale ones fade away.[57] It's about diversifying your friendship portfolio, not cutting off lower-performing investments.

As your belonging archetype evolves, so too should your friendships. They need to expand and embrace a wider range of experiences and perspectives in order to grow. This approach ensures your belonging fuel tank is continually replenished with fresh insights and energy.

How to Make New Friends

Making friends is an essential skill for every archetype but especially if your need for belonging is high. I know it's obvious, but it's important to reiterate: great friendships don't just happen—they are made over time with laughter and tears. Here are three essential factors to improve your ability to form new friendships and deepen existing ones.

Factor #1: Mutual Understanding and Empathy | This skill includes listening, understanding, and empathizing with prospective friends' perspectives and experiences. Being present in conversations means asking meaningful questions and showing genuine interest in what they have to say. Mutual understanding lays the groundwork for bonding and dependability, establishing a secure environment where both sides feel heard and seen.

I often like to think of relationship-building as the continuous act of exchanging sensitive information. Small, vulnerable moments are first shared to test the waters, then as the connection grows and trust is built, more secrets are revealed. When we are honest and open with ourselves in a calm and appropriate manner, it encourages others to do the same and helps to build closer relationships.[58]

Factor #2: Shared Interests, Activities, and Consciousness | Friendships often thrive on shared activities. Engaging in common hobbies, interests, or causes can strengthen bonds and provide regular opportunities for interaction. Whether it's a running buddy, a book club, or a volunteer group, shared activities offer a platform for regular connection and shared experiences. These activities also provide a context in which friendships can grow organically, rooted in mutual passions and pursuits.

Consciousness researcher David R. Hawkins underscores the importance of surrounding ourselves with friends who "vibrate" at similar spiritual levels or have a similar energy level to us.[59] These people not only have similar interests and values, but also interact with the world like we do. This alignment creates a unique sense of belonging based on our shared perspectives on the world we live in.

Factor #3: Consistency and Reliability | Being a reliable friend means showing up when you're needed, literally or figuratively. It's about being consistent in your efforts to connect, whether that's through regular hangouts, texts, or check-ins. Consistency in friendship builds trust and shows that you value the relationship. It also creates a rhythm of interaction that can strengthen the bond over time.

Developing these skills requires practice and the right audience. By continually working on this, you ensure that your friendships remain strong, fulfilling, and deeply aligned with your belonging archetype. And, by regularly meeting new people, you can increase the probability of success in making new friends.

This advice has been around for millennia. The ancient philosopher Aristotle eloquently stated, "A friend is another self." This observation beautifully captures the essence of true friendship—a relationship that mirrors our true selves, providing comfort, understanding, and acceptance without being a carbon copy of us.

Relationships are foundational to belonging, and the longest-running longitudinal study in history—conducted over nearly one hundred years—proves this. The Harvard Study of Adult Development, or the Harvard Longevity Study, began in 1938. It has followed two groups of men for more than eighty years to understand what factors contribute to a long and healthy life. Its most major finding is that people with strong, supportive relationships are happier, healthier, and live longer.

The study's current director, psychiatrist Robert J. Waldinger, says *everybody* needs at least one or two people to count on.[60] When I interviewed him, he added: "Research suggests that the best way to make new relationships is around a shared interest. That could be at work, in some community activity, politics, religion—anywhere where people come together repeatedly and have something in common."[61]

The Flavors of Friendships

When observing Dunbar's Circles, you may have the same question I had: How do I categorize the different people in my life?

The answer lies in understanding the different roles friendships play. *Whole* relationships, found in the concentric circles closest to the center, involve emotional intimacy, trust, and support. These connections require significant time and investment, offering understanding and companionship. They are the relationships we rely on during both crises and celebrations.

Partial relationships, however, fulfill specific roles or needs without deep emotional intimacy. These can be colleagues or casual friends who add to our social circle but don't provide deep emotional satisfaction. While partial relationships may give us a moment of bonding, relying on them can lead to isolation.

Balancing partial and whole relationships is key to a fulfilling social life. Partial relationships introduce diversity and new perspectives, while whole relationships provide the emotional foundation.

You can also view friendships based on how long they last. Three friendship types exist in this context. Some friendships are for a *reason*. They are the short-lived friendships that have a specific benefit; they might "expire" when you get to some sort of realization. The second type is for a *season*. These friendships last for a specific period, perhaps because of a certain circumstance like a breakup or a constraint on your location. Finally, there are friendships for a *lifetime*. These are your forever friends who will be there for you no matter the situation or circumstance.

🪑 COLLECTIVE EXPERIENCES

The second fuel for belonging comes from *collective experiences*. Here we will explore how our involvement in groups, communities, being in a crowd, and even social movements contributes to our sense of belonging.

Groups

Groups are collections of individuals who, while they may have something in common with one another, do not necessarily have a strong connection to each other. Groups are further unique because we may not intentionally join them. This is especially true in

> **Groups are collections of individuals who, while they may have something in common with one another, do not necessarily have a strong connection to each other.**

terms of our demographics. I'm part of the American Jews "group" even though I never actually signed up for it.

When it comes to joining groups, there are also different motivations at play. Sometimes, the motivation is to be an active participant in the group, while other times it's simply to be associated with it (e.g., joining a country club or an alumni association).

How to Select the Right Group

I recognize that the only thing more daunting than finding the right group to join is to be in one that provides zero value. Worse, the wrong one may absolutely drain the energy from you. Here are three best practices I've developed to help you find the right groups to join.

Ensure personal alignment with the community. This includes everything from shared values (e.g., are there any assholes in the group?) to compelling activities (e.g., is this actually matching your needs?). Such alignment will help mitigate potential false positives.

Look for groups that have more than one shared criterion. I call this *the qualifier test*: the more things members have in common with one another, the higher the chances it'll be a good fit. For example, the fact that everyone is a cyclist is not enough to make a cycling group compelling. It's likely to be a better fit if there are other commonalities. Perhaps the group members are all in similar fields, at similar skill levels, or have a shared belief system.

Recognize that it's a numbers game. To find the right group, find multiple options and practice due diligence. Finding the right group is a two-way street, so be prepared to explore many options before discovering the one that fills your fuel tank. Fail fast and often, without any hard feelings.

Participating in a group, whether it's a Facebook group, a meetup for corgis, a sports team, or a subreddit, fills up our belonging tank and may give us a sense of fulfillment. However, the stakes are generally lower than the commitment required to join a community.

Many groups are often mislabeled as communities, oftentimes in a manipulative manner, in order to make them sound more appealing and sentimental. Nevertheless, communities are a distinct form of collective experiences with specific criteria.

Communities

It's easy to notice that the word "community" is overused these days. It's become so commonplace that I find myself rolling my eyes whenever I see it mentioned. For this reason, I want to be exceptionally intentional when using the word, and a good place to start is by referring to the experts.

In the academic definition by psychologists David W. McMillan and David M. Chavis, community is defined as "a social unit formed by relational bonds where members share common values, interests, or identity and have a sense of belonging, a level of influence, and emotional connection."[62]

Here are the four criteria that they say contribute to this *sense of community*:[63]

- **Membership**. You need to have a sense that members have invested time, effort, and other resources to be part of the group, thereby gaining a "right to belong."

This investment fosters emotional security and psychological safety.

- **Influence**. Members need to affect the group's decisions and actions while also being shaped by the group. This interdependence encourages active participation. If the group values their input, members are more likely to contribute positively.

- **Reinforcement**. A positive feedback loop is crucial to successful communities so that members find it beneficial and rewarding to engage. When the members' needs are met, it reinforces their commitment and satisfaction, and the community flywheel gets activated.

- **Shared emotional connection**. Emotional bonds are strengthened through rituals, traditions, and shared experiences, deepening the unity for all involved.

In summary, a community has members that invest their resources in it, allows for members to influence it, creates engagement loops within it, and unlocks emotional bonds through shared experiences.

Richard Millington, a community expert, created a taxonomy that identifies five categories of how people form communities. I added a sixth. These communities are defined by the underlying purposes that unite their members, ranging from shared interests to life circumstances.[64] Although not comprehensive, this categorization will suffice to identify the most suitable groups for you.

- **Community of Interest.** Communities where people gather based on shared hobbies or pursuits.

- **Community of Action.** Communities where people come together to accomplish a specific mission or goal.

- **Community of Practice.** Communities where people share a profession or practice and come together to improve their skills and knowledge.

- **Community of Place.** Communities formed around a geographic location or physical space where people live or meet regularly.

- **Community of Circumstance.** Communities where people are brought together by a shared situation or life experience.

- **Community of Belief.** Communities formed around shared beliefs or ideologies.

How to Experiment with Starting a Community

If starting a community sounds like a lot of work, fret not; there are lower effort ways to get some of the same benefits without as much commitment or risk. One point that may alleviate your concerns is that you do not need to be friends with everyone that participates. Think of it as another relationship, except to a collective instead of an individual.

Create a text group around a shared topic. Sometimes, starting a community can be as easy as creating a text chain or a WhatsApp group. Simply gather several people who are interested in the same thing and start sharing resources like articles, links, memes, or posts. This kind of low friction group can eventually lead to deeper connections and to community.

Organize a small event. You may have noticed that groups naturally form after a shared group experience (e.g., the wedding group chat continues well after the wedding has concluded). This social bonding occurs naturally because of the individuals' shared past. One low-risk way to create such a community is to organize a small event. Nick Gray, the author of *The 2-Hour Cocktail Party*, told me that hosting a small meetup or happy hour is the best way to meet interesting people and build or grow your network. The only piece of advice I have, apart from reading his book, is to consider how to make the space welcoming for every one of the belonging archetypes that may be in attendance.

Start a book club. A book club is an excellent way to bring like-minded people together regularly—not just to socialize, but also to learn together. Over time, these discussions can lead to stronger relationships and a sense of community among members.

While all communities are groups, most groups are not communities. The best communities are said to be the ones where members experience high levels of social cohesion, which is best characterized by—you guessed it—a sense of belonging.[65]

Differences between men and women are an important consideration when it comes to considering groups and communities as belonging fuel. A study by professors William W. Maddux and Marilynn B. Brewer found that men develop trust based on shared group memberships, while women trust through direct or indirect relationship connections.[66] Another study by psychologists Shira Gabriel and Wendi L. Gardner found men prefer activities that involve larger groups. In contrast, women are more likely to engage in groups where they can build personal relationships.[67]

Being in a Crowd

The collective experience path extends beyond group membership to encompass being part of crowds at events and large gatherings. The concept of *collective effervescence* was first coined by sociologist Émile Durkheim. It captures the exhilarating sense of connection we feel in a crowd, like a concert, religious gathering, political rally, or live sports event. This is where we feel the strength of our collective identity and the unity that comes from being part of a greater whole. These moments transcend individual identity,

These moments transcend individual identity, creating a shared emotional experience that fosters a powerful sense of belonging.

creating a shared emotional experience that fosters a powerful sense of belonging.[68]

When people share an experience, their brain waves synchronize. The experience of "being on the same wavelength" as someone else is real and observable in brain activity. Just like dancers moving in perfect unison, the neurons in corresponding locations of different people's brains fire simultaneously, creating matching patterns.[69]

Throughout history, humans have sought experiences that unite them as a collective. These gatherings blur the lines between ourselves and others. A study led by social psychologist Daniel A. Yudkin showed that participants who engage in these experiences can expect long-lasting positive effects.[70]

Yudkin's team tracked attendees at a variety of secular, large-scale gatherings in the US and UK. Their findings validated what you've likely intuited about these events. During the gatherings, the study found that "participants experienced feelings of universal connectedness and developed new perceptions of others." Six months after the gatherings, attendees self-reported being more generous and showed signs of an expanded sense of morality.[71]

For anyone who has been to an event with music, visuals, or dancing, you have most likely experienced something similar. Sharing from personal experience, one aspect of raves and music festivals that has always stood out to me is their unparalleled ability to foster connections among attendees. At a festival, each corner brings a fresh chance to interact—whether it's discovering new artists, making unexpected connections, or being captivated by art installations. These instances are not merely coincidental but deliberate invitations for individuals to find their place within a broader temporary community.

If you're inclined to pursue this fuel but don't know where to start, check out camping festivals like Shambala, Bonnaroo, Lightning in a Bottle, or Electric Forest instead of urban-based festivals like Lollapalooza. And don't let the fear of going alone hold you back—these festivals have online forums with subgroups for making solo attendance safe and inviting.

Social Movements

The collective experience fuel extends to include social movements. Being involved in a cause you believe in, whether it's marching in a rally or holding a protest sign, allows you to find a sense of belonging. From labor union organizing to the civil rights movement, this path has been significant in our country's modern history.

This pattern becomes particularly evident when a segment of society experiences heightened loneliness. This was seen during the BLM protests, which occurred at the peak of mass isolation during the global pandemic. It is also reflected in the high energy at Trump rallies, where many attendees feel they are being left behind.

The recent anti-Israel demonstrations of 2024 are another example of this kind of convergence. Given the mental health challenges of today's college students, it's not surprising that the Israel-Hamas war has united many of them. As one Columbia

University student said about her school's protests, "Lonely students found an inviting community of support inside demonstrations and the [Gaza] encampment on the quad."[72]

CASUAL ENCOUNTERS

The third and final traditional path is founded through the many interactions we are consistently having throughout our days. I call these *casual encounters*. These microinteractions may be brief and seemingly inconsequential, but together they profoundly affect our sense of belonging. These are the small moments of connection we share with acquaintances, neighbors, or even strangers.

Strangers

Consider the friendly honk to a neighbor, the small talk with your barista who knows what your "usual" is, or the GIF exchanges in a Slack chat room. These interactions, though brief, carry weight. No matter how small they are, they remind us of our humanity. According to research by psychology professors Jennifer Hirsch and Margaret Clark, "merely connecting briefly with others, being pleasantly social with them, and receiving pleasant responses from them [contribute] to a sense of belonging."[73]

When I first moved to Boise, people told me, "There's nice, and there's Boise nice." There is even a "Keep Boise Kind" billboard on a main thoroughfare in town and "Be Kind" signs on trails. I didn't know what these meant at first, but when a cop abruptly stopped me to chat about DC (he saw my car's license plates) I got the hint. Now, I jump to be the first to greet people on trails or neighborhood walks. The act of greeting strangers has made me feel like I belong here, and I recommend you give it a shot.

Casual encounters are beautiful because of their ripple effect. A simple smile or a kind exchange can brighten someone's day, spreading positivity and shaping the recipient's future interactions. This ripple effect can spread far beyond the initial contact, creating a network of positivity. It's a reminder that even the smallest gesture can contribute to a greater sense of life satisfaction, both for ourselves and those around us.[74]

How to Become a Regular

A simple way you can build relationships with others is to frequent the same locations. Becoming a regular in certain spaces is more than just showing up often; it's about being recognized as part of the environment.

The idea of a "third place" is crucial in a hybrid world where individuals work from both the home and the office. Third places like coffee shops, parks, and coworking spaces provide a vital setting for social interaction. They offer a sense of community that can help combat the isolation of remote work and the lack of regular life routines.[75] An added perk of occupying third places is that it can help jumpstart your interpersonal relationship fuel with exposure to fellow regulars, if you're so inclined.

Acquaintances

Some people have a propensity to have many acquaintances in their outermost circles while others can't. If you can catch up with an old friend every few months and quickly achieve a certain level of intimacy without much of a warm-up, I'm talking to you. This propensity to have many people in this category is a personal preference based in part off our psychological profile, so only you can know what works for you. It is through this subfuel that the special powers of your archetype can shine and where Dunbar's Circles start to be more of an art than a science.

Now that we've reviewed the different traditional fuels, let's move into nontraditional fuels, which create similar results when it comes to influencing our sense of belonging.

DEAR FELLOW BELONGING SEEKER:

If this book is serving you, please consider leaving a positive Amazon review to help others discover this book so that they too can find their sense of belonging.

Thank you so much for reading and helping me get the word out.

—Dan

CHAPTER 8

UNCOVERING NONTRADITIONAL BELONGING PATHS

"In reading great literature I become a
thousand men and yet remain myself."
—C.S. LEWIS

Set in Birmingham, England, the BBC Two crime drama series *Peaky Blinders* is one of my favorite shows of all time. From the first episode, I was captivated by the cinematography, artistic design, and costumes. I connected with the cast of diverse characters, regardless of their motives or flaws. And I was swept away by the complex and intricate stories that the show told. I spent many evenings binge-watching a handful of episodes only to hop on the show's subreddit to continue indulging my infatuation with fellow fans.

Whenever I saw the main character Thomas Shelby, played by Cillian Murphy, let out a cloud of smoke, I found myself craving cigarette. And when he imbibed a drink of whiskey, I felt the urge to pour myself a glass as if I were by his side. When a scene came on with the Jewish gangster Alfie Solomons, played by Tom Hardy, I felt an immediate affinity to him because of our shared heritage, despite the fact he could be quite cruel. And when Helen McCrory, who played Polly Gray, the matriarch of the Shelby family, lost her battle with cancer in real life, I mourned her death alongside the show's cast.

I loved *Peaky Blinders* so much that I lovingly forced my wife to rewatch every one of the six seasons with me. It never got old, and that says a lot for someone with ADHD.

By now you might be wondering why I'm sharing this with you and what it has to do with belonging.

The answer is that symbolic bonds, like the one I formed with Tommy and other fictional characters on the show, are one of several nontraditional paths to finding belonging. Here we will explore this broad category which also includes esteem-building fuels and contemplative practices.

SYMBOLIC BONDS

These connections can come from fictional characters, nonfictional personas, or inanimate objects.

The symbolic bonds fuel highlights the emotional connection we get from people and things we cannot physically interact with. These connections can come from fictional characters, nonfictional personas, or inanimate objects. While further research needs to be conducted to deduce whether this kind of social surrogacy suppresses belonging needs or actually fulfills them, it is still a legitimate path given the perceived outcome it has on individuals.[76]

Parasocial Relationships

One-sided relationships are referred to as *parasocial relationships*. This path is about our ability to form meaningful connections with fictional characters in books, TV shows, movies, and video games. Though not real in the physical sense, these characters become part of our lives, influencing our emotions, thoughts, and sometimes even our actions. They can even give us companionship.[77]

This fuel becomes particularly fascinating in a world filled with influencers, creators, streamers, and YouTubers, where individuals devote their emotional energy, interest, and time to someone who is completely unaware of their existence. This is in no way a new phenomenon. In ancient Rome, for example, gladiators were revered and idolized in a similar way. Social media has just made this behavior even more mainstream.

Comfort Artifacts and Mementos

Much like parasocial relationships, listening to music, consuming comfort foods, looking at old photos, interacting with memorabilia, and rereading sentimental letters can also trigger powerful feelings of connection to specific memories of or moments with loved ones.[78] These bonds provide a sense of continuity and comfort, linking us to cherished memories and emotions.

You may have noticed that chefs on cooking shows frequently discuss what the dish they are preparing reminds them of—Sunday dinners, Thanksgiving, or grandma's cooking. These comfort foods are a proxy for the important relationships these chefs have in their lives.

Similarly, listening to music from the era in which you grew up evokes stronger emotions than merely listening to a new album by any artist. The same effect can be felt when listening to a track you heard during a sunrise set on repeat.

ESTEEM-BUILDING

For our purposes, esteem-building is characterized by activities and pursuits aimed at gaining others' approval or admiration. While seeking affirmation may be scrutinized by judgmental critics, the fuel sheds light on how our desire for acceptance from others significantly impacts our sense of belonging.

> While seeking affirmation may be scrutinized by judgmental critics, the fuel sheds light on how our desire for acceptance from others significantly impacts our sense of belonging.

Validation and Recognition

It's hard to imagine life without constant, reassuring feedback loops. This underlying drive manifests in various ways, such as achieving success in your career, maintaining a high standing in society, or possessing nice things. It's the pursuit of symbols and actions that signal our worth and success to others. Naturally, it encompasses all the social media metrics we strive for, such as likes, views, followers, and fans. Ultimately, the drive behind all these "superficial" desires for validation is to be recognized and admired, which feeds our sense of belonging.

When I was just entering the dating world, I put a lot of weight on the physical appearance of the women I was seeing. The truth is that I was doing it to seek validation from others. A study conducted by Mark Snyder and colleagues primarily observed this behavior in men. The emphasis on the physical attractiveness of their romantic partners is linked to their strong social motivation.[79] Embarrassingly, it was just another way for me to feel accepted.

Status Objects

Chasing attractiveness can also carry over to materialism. When I moved to Idaho, I spent a lot of money on acquiring possessions that are considered textbook "Idahoan," such as a pickup truck. Studies have confirmed that materialism can serve as a response to feelings of not fitting in, uncertainty, and belonginglessness.[80] Buying gear and bagging experiences were my coping mechanisms for social insecurity, giving me a false sense of control over my newly forming identity.

This fuel is "convenient" because it does not require showing up vulnerably; in fact, it doesn't require any deep relationships. Researchers have found that individuals who lack intimate relationships might use material possessions as a substitute for genuine interpersonal connections.[81]

One example is the MAGA movement's merchandise—its red hats, Trump flags, and "Let's go Brandon" signs. Much like brand-name fashion and high-end electronics, owning and displaying this swag allows the ideology's followers to use these material goods to create a visible identity. This visible identity provides a sense of belonging through the owner's association with the movement.

Pet Ownership

Caring for pets is another subfuel within the broad self-esteem path. Multiple studies have shown that pet ownership decreases loneliness and increases self-esteem.[82] In fact, one study showed that simply thinking about our pets can alleviate our mood after we experience rejection.[83] So yes, get all the puppies.

The journey to building self-esteem can have its drawbacks. On the one hand, it can boost our sense of achievement and social integration, positively filling our belonging fuel tank. On the other, it can lead to a constant chase for external validation. Unironically, I recognize that writing a book is an esteem-building activity in and of itself. I would be lying if I said that, in sharing my insights and experiences, I don't seek to gain recognition for helping people.

CONTEMPLATIVE PRACTICES

Contemplative practices such as prayer, meditation, transcendence, introspection, and spending time in nature form the last path. These fuels allow us to connect more deeply with ourselves or with something beyond ourselves, like a higher power or the natural world.

> **These fuels allow us to connect more deeply with ourselves or with something beyond ourselves, like a higher power or the natural world.**

Prayer

The spiritual teacher Sadhguru says that prayer is "asking God to do something" while meditation is simply "shutting up" and accepting what comes.[84] Therein lies the difference between the two contemplative practices.

Prayer, when taken literally, is not about introspection. It's about communicating with a higher power. If connecting with the divine on your own or through a religious gathering is a way you find belonging, then this fuel is right for you.

Meditation and Introspection

When you revisit Sadhguru's definition of meditation, you'll notice a subtle message about the existence of God. In saying that meditation is about "accepting what comes," he leaves space for God's will. By surrendering, we're neither acknowledging nor rejecting God's existence. When it comes to contemplative practices, there is room for both prayer and meditation.

How to Start Meditating

Meditation is not about completely disconnecting or controlling the mind. You are not imposing something on your mind too forcefully nor are you letting it wander. It is the practice of letting the mind be.[85]

Various types of meditation can assist you in achieving this goal, and with practice you will improve regardless of the specific method you choose. If you are interested in exploring meditation, here are six common types to consider:

- **Mindfulness.** Awareness of the present moment using modalities such as breathwork and tools such as a body scan.

- **Loving-Kindness.** Development of compassion toward self and others.

- **Vipassana.** Observation of thoughts without attachment or judgement.

- **Mantra-Based Meditation.** Repetition of a mantra with the goal of transcending. A common practice is Transcendental Meditation (TM).

- **Guided Meditation.** Relaxation through wisdom shared by teachers leveraging different modalities such as visualizations, sounds, and scents.

- **Movement Meditation.** Achieving a sense of calm through physical activity, such as walking meditation, yoga, or tai chi.

Research by a team led by psychologist Stephanie Dorais supports integrating meditations into your wellness routine. During a four-week period, participants who practiced a mantra-based meditation saw significant improvements in their ability to recover from challenges. Such resilience is a foundational quality for anyone working to move past their traumas and find a sense of belonging.[86]

To understand the beautiful connection between meditation and belonging, I asked my meditation teacher, Laurent Valosek, for help. He explained that when a feeling of inner peace is achieved through meditation, our state of consciousness is elevated. As our consciousness rises, so does our ability to simply be and to perceive the world's interconnectedness with exceptional clarity. An interconnected world is a world where no one is othered. When it comes to humanity, everyone belongs.

When it comes to humanity, everyone belongs.

Introspection doesn't only come from meditation. It can also come from the simple act of journaling. Social psychologist James W. Pennebaker has studied how expressive writing can help with therapeutic processes. People who write about their emotions better understand and process them. This kind of contemplation can enhance our self-esteem and facilitate emotional regulation.[87] These benefits allow us to show up as our best selves in social situations.

Exploration and Wonder

The practice of cultivating awe is a significant aspect of the contemplative practice path as well. Awe is the emotion that arises when we witness something immense and extraordinary that challenges our perception of reality. You can achieve this by traveling to unique places, finding inspiration in natural environments, or experiencing different cultures. Or you could do this by observing the vast night sky or studying the complexity of a symphony.

The Netflix documentary *Fantastic Fungi* teaches us about interconnectedness through the lens of mycelium, a root-like structure of fungi. In my interview with one of the featured experts in the film, Paul Stamets, a renowned author of eight mushroom-related books, he described mycelium as "the Earth's natural internet." Mycelia, he explained, create interconnected nodes resembling synapses in our brain, which come together to form an expansive web that surrounds us in ways we can hardly fathom.[88] He told me that mycelium decomposes organic matter and rejuvenates hostile habitats—it's present where life begins and where it ends.

This illustrates how there is beauty, wonder, and an ever-evolving curiosity to be found whenever we stop to look. This concept is captured in something called the *overview effect*, a term used to describe the significant change in perspective that astronauts feel when they see Earth from space. More technically, it's defined as "a state of awe with self-transcendent qualities, precipitated by a particularly striking visual stimulus."[89]

Experiencing awe shifts our focus away from ourselves and our individual concerns, connecting us with the grandeur of the human experience and the universe as a whole. This shift can be incredibly grounding, reminding us that we are part of something much larger than anything we can possibly imagine, an idea that Ray Dalio captures very eloquently:

It is a reality that each one of us is only one of about seven billion of our species alive today and that our species is only one of about ten million species on our planet. Earth is just one of about 100 billion planets in our galaxy, which is just one of about two trillion galaxies in the universe. And our lifetimes are only about 1/3,000 of humanity's existence, which itself is only 1/20,000 of the Earth's existence. In other words, we are unbelievably tiny and short-lived....[90]

Contemplative practices encompass our connection to ourselves, our awareness, and our relationship with everything around us, including nature and the universe. It invites us to explore the depths of our being, to seek moments of wonder throughout nature, and to connect with the vastness of existence. This fuel serves as a reminder that, despite our current emotions, we are not alone in our journey of belonging.

THE FULL BELONGING TAXONOMY

While we tend to rely on a few fuels for our sense of belonging, it is possible to mix and match different sources, especially if we have a strong need to feel connected.

Mixing fuels can either enhance the efficiency of something or result in spontaneous combustion. The same is true for our belonging fuels. Take the example of winning a championship with a sports team. Winning can boost players' self-esteem and strengthen their friendships. These two paths complement each other. Recognition leads to stronger relationships, and stronger relationships can lead to even better outcomes.

On the flip side, working around the clock to seek validation from a manager may cause someone to neglect their communal relationships. This conflict can lead someone to sacrifice deep personal connections for professional success. Heed caution and confirm fuel compatibility.

Here is the list of all the fuels and subfuels we've covered:

 ## Interpersonal Relationships

- ❯ Romantic partner
- ❯ Family
- ❯ Close friends

 ## Collective Experiences

- ❯ Groups
- ❯ Communities

- ❯ Being in a crowd
- ❯ Social movements

 ## Casual Encounters

- ❯ Strangers
- ❯ Acquaintances

 ## Symbolic Bonds

- ❯ Comfort artifacts and mementos
- ❯ Emotional connections to fictional characters
- ❯ Parasocial (one-sided) relationships

 ## Esteem-Building

- ❯ Validation and recognition
- ❯ Status objects
- ❯ Pet ownership

 ## Contemplative Practices

- ❯ Prayer
- ❯ Meditation
- ❯ Journaling
- ❯ Exploration and wonder

Complete this digitally at belongingquest.com/exercises

INTERMEDIATE BELONGING FUEL TANK

No.	Activity	Percentage
1		
2		
3		
4		
5		
6		
7		
8		
9		
10		
11		

It's time to upgrade our belonging fuel tank. This next version should take into consideration all the personalized strategies that align with the requirements and preferences of your archetype. For meerkats and chimps, it's likely quantity over quality. For snow leopards and wolves, it's quality over quantity. And for some, it could be both.

1. Pull up the last version of your tank.

2. Remove any activities that no longer resonate with you because:

    a. You've become aware that they don't match your belonging archetype.

    b. They're a false summit (hand-me-down, nostalgic, or misconceived fuels that don't actually serve you).

3. Incorporate any fuels that were not previously on your radar.

4. Reallocate the percentages.

5. Add up the percentages. What's their sum? (Keep in mind, empty space is an opportunity for exploration and personal development!)

This revised version of your fuel tank should look and feel much more authentic to your archetype. This congruent pursuit of activities and relationships that foster connection is what intentional belonging is all about.

Unintentional Belonging

Before The Quest there was cognitive
dissonance between who you are and how
you sought belonging.

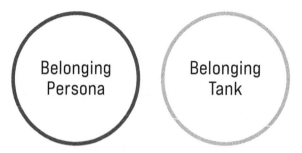

Intentional Belonging

As a result of The Quest there is cognitive
consistency between your belonging
persona and belonging tank.

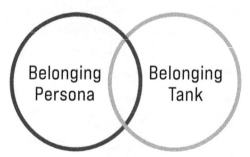

CHAPTER 9
LIGHTENING THE LOAD

"Contrary to popular belief, winners quit
a lot. That's how they win."
—ANNIE DUKE

At the beginning of 2024, I realized that the sheer number of commitments I had made to various membership groups was overwhelming. As someone who always puts in full effort, I felt ashamed that I wasn't actively participating in many of them. Normally, I would have pushed myself to increase my capacity, but this time I decided to try something different. I set a goal to leave most of these organizations.

Over the next few months, I began stepping down from leadership positions, declining invitations, and resigning from groups where I wasn't fully engaged. The result was a breath of fresh air—not just in terms of reduced guilt but also in terms of having more room in my belonging tank for my family and the exploration of new hobbies.

One of those hobbies was a throwback to my high school days: video games. I used to play first-person shooters and real-time strategy games competitively with friends I met online in the late '90s. This hobby wasn't just about the games; it involved building the gaming machine, optimizing its setup, and connecting with fellow gamers.

At the age of forty-two, I reunited with my gamer friends and returned to a hobby I had left over twenty years ago. It has felt so good to come back to something that I enjoy, that has a community around it, and that I can do on my own without any external pressure.

It's funny to think about how being intentional about finding my sense of belonging has taken so long, but I really welcome it. Now, it's your turn.

At this point, you not only know your belonging archetype, but you have also learned about the six different fuels at your disposal to find belonging. It's time to see how the two come together to form a more customized version of your tank. Intentional belonging starts now.

INTENTIONAL BELONGING

Below are archetype-specific fuel recommendations to help customize The Quest for the person that you are. If you have a blended archetype, whereby you are on or near the border of a secondary archetype, feel free to mix and match what might work for you.

 Interpersonal Relationships

 Collective Experiences

 Casual Encounters

 Symbolic Bonds

 Esteem-Building

 Contemplative Practices

For Chimps (Eager)

Chimps are constantly seeking ways to fill their belonging fuel tank through myriads of activities to satisfy their high need to belong. Because of their secure attachment style, they have deep relationships and a healthy balance of independence and closeness. If you're a chimp, try prioritizing these four fuels:

- **Interpersonal relationships**. Maintain close relationships with friends and family, including finding the right romantic partner, to satisfy your high need to belong.

- **Collective experiences**, especially communities that reinforce your social circles; consider starting groups where you can set the tone for engagement to broaden your fuel intake and give you recognition.

- **Casual encounters**. Engage in regular, friendly interactions with neighbors, acquaintances, and colleagues to ensure consistent social engagement.

- **Esteem-building**. Strive for achievements in a personal or professional field to boost your self-esteem through public acknowledgment.

For Meerkats (Anxious)

Like chimps, meerkats are eager for belonging, but unlike chimps, they don't always feel secure in having it. This is why they might find themselves trying new fuels and maybe even overcommitting to too many fuels. A staple of their archetype is the need for continuous feedback and affirmation. If you're a meerkat, try the following fuels out:

- **Interpersonal relationships.** Develop several close, reassuring relationships, especially with a securely attached partner to strengthen your disposition as someone who has an insecure attachment style. The unconditional bond formed from having a family may also be very powerful for you.

- **Collective experiences**, especially events and large gatherings to prevent feelings of isolation by experiencing shared emotional connections within the safety of a crowd. You may also benefit from over-indexing on digital groups to alleviate social anxiety.

- **Symbolic bonds**, especially comfort artifacts and mementos. Reconnecting with meaningful people through tapping into sentimental memories might provide helpful reassurance as you need it.

- **Esteem-building.** Different paths that provide recognition and validation, from having a following online to boosting your social standing, may help improve your self-esteem.

- **Contemplative practice.** Any of the pursuits in this fuel will work well to reduce reactivity, slow you down, and help you develop a more secure sense of self.

For Snow Leopards (Reluctant)

Due to their low need for social connection and insecure attachment style, snow leopards prefer minimal social contact. They exhibit caution getting close to people and show reluctance in enthusiastically joining. If you're a snow leopard, here are three fuels for your consideration:

- **Symbolic bonds**, especially parasocial relationships whereby you engage with fictional characters. You might find that they provide a sense of safety and comfort to fulfill some social needs without the associated risk of rejection.

- **Casual encounters**. Instead of maintaining too many deep relationships, focusing on your acquaintances will get you the benefits of social interactions without the pressure.

- **Communal association**, specifically online forums or chat rooms where you can have controlled engagements that happen on your terms and consider your boundaries.

For Wolves (Independent)

The wolf's belonging fuel tank is steady. Due to their secure attachment and low need for belonging, they prioritize meaningful connections over extensive social engagements. If you're a wolf, here are my suggestions:

- **Interpersonal relationships**. Maintain a few strong, reliable, and intimate relationships, including a primary romantic one, that provide meaningful connections without overwhelming your need for independence.

- **Symbolic bonds**. Have several fictional outlets, like books or shows, that help you feel connection when you wish to be left alone.

- **Contemplative practice**, specifically journaling and immersion in the natural world around you, to connect with yourself more deeply.

- **Validation and recognition**, specifically focusing on mastery within any of your inherent talents or learned crafts.

THE FIVE C'S FOR EVALUATING YOUR FUELS

As you were crafting your intermediate belonging tank and you were focusing on intentionality, you may have questioned some activities' effectiveness or relevance. To help you critically assess them, here are five questions, which I call the Five C's, to help you out:

- **Certainty**. Instinctively, do you feel like this strategy serves you? This is a gut check because, more times than not, our intuition knows the truth.

- **Charged**. Does participating in this activity make you feel energized? We don't want to do anything that is energy draining.

- **Connected**. Is it possible for you to show up genuinely when participating in this strategy? Remember, you can't feel belonging unless you can be yourself.

- **Celebrated**. Do you take pride in participating in it? Broadcasting your participation is a key indicator that the activity aligns with your values.

- **Championed**. Would you recommend it to others like you? A strong endorsement signals that the activity is impactful for you.

If you responded negatively to any of these questions, then the strategy in question may not be a wise investment of your time or resources. Think about pausing, revising, or eliminating it entirely from your tank to create room for another strategy.

BEING INTENTIONAL ABOUT COLLECTIVE EXPERIENCES

At the beginning of this chapter, I mentioned my goal to shed many of the groups I was affiliated with. I had amassed these groups because, as someone who craves belonging and has struggled with attachment, I've always sought a collective to fill a void. To decide which groups to keep and which to leave, I devised a basic evaluation of all the things that fall under the collective experience fuel.

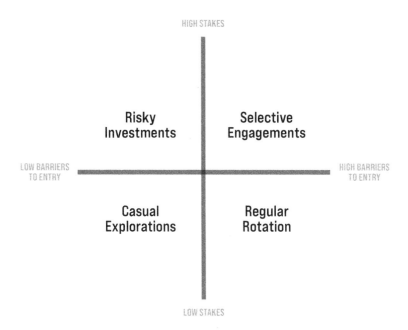

Risky Investments. Stay away from the groups that over-promise and underdeliver.

Expensive Conferences, Luxury Gyms or High-End Exercise Classes, Guru Masterminds

Selective Engagements. Research closely and do a few at a time.

Multi-day Festivals, Industry Meetings, Membership (e.g. Country Club), Business Groups

Casual Explorations. Do as many as you wish with low expectations and leave quickly when not serving you.

Facebook Groups, Discord Servers

Regular Rotation. Do lots of these in order to find which works best for you.

Meetups, Rec Leagues, Book Club

The top left section includes the risky investments. These are the communities, events, and groups that are high stakes and open to everyone. Essentially, these investments have no other unique aspect besides being seen as exclusive. While they claim to offer a one-of-a-kind experience, anyone who pays a significant amount of money can become a member. My general advice is to steer clear of these groups. They may appear fun on social media or in marketing materials, but they make big promises and frequently fail to deliver.

The bottom left quadrant is for *casual explorations*. Exploring these communities is a breeze since many are online and have open access with low requirements. However, because they are not restricted, the level of involvement might be lacking, and the quality of interactions might be poor. You can explore these groups, but it's crucial to have realistic expectations about the value they offer and to leave them promptly if they cannot meet your expectations.

The bottom right quadrant contains any community on *regular rotation*. With their limited availability and minimal requirements, these offer a fair chance to engage meaningfully without needing many resources. These groups are great for people who want to make close connections and participate in regular activities without the pressure of being in exclusive groups. I suggest exploring numerous options to identify those most suitable to you.

Finally, the top right quadrant is for *selective engagements*. It is recommended to limit attendance at these groups and gatherings, as they typically have strict entry requirements due to their exclusivity. Joining these groups can be beneficial, but it's crucial to approach them cautiously, considering the time, money, and commitment involved.

With this improved evaluation process, I hope you can make smarter decisions about where to invest your time and resources to make a positive impact on your sense of belonging.

EXERCISE *Complete this digitally at belongingquest.com/exercises*

ADVANCED BELONGING FUEL TANK

No.	Activity	Percentage
1		
2		
3		
4		
5		
6		
7		
8		
9		
10		
11		

It's time to make one final revision to your belonging fuel tank. The key to this process is to critically analyze which strategies to maintain, strengthen, or abandon. A secondary goal is to approach it as our ideal tank—something we can refer to well after we've completed The Quest.

1. Pull up the last version of your tank.
2. Adjust any strategies that may or may not fit now that you understand your archetype's intentional fuels.
3. Reconsider any activities that do not pass the Five C's.
4. Reconsider any collective experiences that no longer serve you.
5. Reallocate the percentages. Try and set higher percentages for your favorite activities so that this version becomes a more idealistic representation of how you aspire to find belonging.
6. Add up the percentages. What's their sum?

Again, any empty space in your tank is a chance for exploration—a skill I'll help you enhance once we reach the summit. In fact, a 100-percent-full tank leaves no room for creativity, innovation, or excitement.

Given that some strategies that didn't serve you were removed, you might observe that this third and final version of your tank is leaner than previous versions. Or it might be fuller since this is more of an ideal fuel tank than previous iterations. Regardless, it is now yours to build upon and enhance. Congratulations. You're clear to proceed to the summit.

STAGE IV
SUMMIT

CHAPTER 10

SCANNING THE HORIZON

"Your life does not get better by chance; it gets better by change."
—JIM ROHN

Back in March 2020, I was stuck in my DC apartment, waiting for COVID-19 to blow over so I could finally move back to NYC. At least that was the plan. I had just left Social Tables and was ready to return to my hometown after being away for more than a decade. But cabin fever hit hard, and I needed to get out of my small apartment to pass the time during lockdown until such a move was possible.

What was supposed to be a quick getaway turned into a three-month, fifteen-thousand-mile, cross-country road trip. This experience became the driving force behind my own voyage and, ultimately, resulted in me writing this book. My friends and I weaved our way through nearly half of the lower continental states and slept in eighteen unique cities. Toward the end of the trip, on our way to Bozeman, Montana, from Salt Lake City, Utah, we made a detour to Boise, Idaho.

At first, I didn't find the flat, seemingly uninhabited state impressive. But as we began to get closer to Boise, I noticed the beautiful foothills of the Treasure Valley, and my attitude changed. We rolled up to a cheap hotel, dropped our stuff off, and headed downtown. I was immediately struck by how nice everyone we encountered was. As we spent more time in the City of Trees, its majesty—from its hundreds of miles of wilderness trails to the seemingly unlimited opportunities for recreation—set in. After a few days, I stored those memories away, and we got back on the road to head south.

By the end of June, with just a few weeks remaining on our trip, tensions were running high as my friends and I were starting to annoy each other. As we drove on what felt like an endless road, staring at the forever-setting Texas sun, I remember thinking to myself that I could move anywhere I wanted because of my unique circumstances.

I was jobless and single, so why had I not considered options other than NYC? What was behind my desire to go back to the safety of a city I had already experienced for most of my teens and twenties? What if I did a complete one-eighty and moved somewhere completely unexpected?

And what if that place was Boise?

To settle into my new city, I had to change my focus and prioritize my personal well-being over my work, something they don't teach you on the East Coast. Being in a smaller city, people in Boise place lifestyle and family over career advancement and professional success. This makes it more of a "work to live" type of place rather than a "live to work" type of city. I had to slow down and stop trying to bring *there* here.

Welcome to the **summit**. Here, we have a different vantage point. Our first order of business is to scan the horizon, see what's ahead, and look down at what remains below. Here we will answer the critical question that remains: How is our environment influencing our sense of belonging, and what can we do about it?

> **How is our environment influencing our sense of belonging, and what can we do about it?**

THE VIEW FROM ABOVE

The various stable and semi-stable circumstances in our life make up our **belonging environment**. These circumstances influence our sense of belonging because they can either constrict or expand the opportunities that come our way. They include our cultural identity, geographic location, overall health, relationship status, education level, employment stability, socioeconomic status, and our consciousness level.

Take, for example, where we live. A chimp would have a hard time living in a remote place without many opportunities for the constant interactions they thrive on. Similarly, a snow leopard wouldn't be their best self in a communal living facility.

Environmental factors are responsible for up to 10 percent of our overall happiness.[91] Although 10 percent may seem small, it's important to consider it in context. We know that 40 percent of our happiness comes from the intentional activities we engage in. Together, these two components are responsible for 50 percent of our overall happiness, the same proportion that our genetic set point plays. With this small but mighty slice, we now have a ball game!

Let's explore each one of these variables in more depth to see where you might have an unfair advantage and to be even more intentional about how you find belonging.

CULTURAL IDENTITY

Your main cultural identity, whether it is based on ethnicity, race, or religion, influences the rituals you may engage in, the places where you worship, and the people you choose to be around. These social and spiritual experiences provide numerous opportunities to enhance a sense of belonging.

I didn't realize how important my Jewish identity was to me until I moved to a place without many Jews. That's when I leaned in and started being a lot more curious about Judaism and a little more observant of its traditions. This made my wife think about the advantages of embracing the same culture and religion, including its values, perspectives, and customs. With her initiation of the conversion process, our family's dedication to the same tradition has bolstered my sense of belonging even more than when it was just me.

What role does your cultural identity play in how you find belonging? How is it helping or hindering?

GEOGRAPHY

Where you live, particularly your location, plays a fundamental role in shaping your sense of belonging as it impacts your social interactions and opportunities to engage with diverse communities. A suitable environment consists of settings, people, and situations that deeply resonate with your belonging archetype. If you find yourself in the wrong environment, your chances for meaningful interactions will be restricted.

Moving to a different place can be like hitting a reset button on your sense of belonging, giving you the chance to explore new options and expand your horizons. "Where you live largely determines who you know," writes the serial entrepreneur and venture capitalist James Currier, and "who you know largely determines the richness of [and access in] your life." The social network created by location is a form of wealth that "brings you friends, career opportunities, or a spouse."[92]

In an article published in the *Atlantic* in 1996, Nicholas Lemann noted from his personal experiences that residents of larger cities tend to prioritize their professional lives, resulting in less time dedicated to their community. Lemann writes:

> *I have lived in five American cities: New Orleans, Cambridge, Washington, Austin, and Pelham, New York. The two that stand out in my memory as most deficient in the Putnam virtues—the places where people I know tend not to have elaborate hobbies and not to devote their evenings and weekends to neighborhood meetings and activities—are Cambridge and Washington. The reason is that these places are the big time. Work absorbs all the energy. It is what people talk about at social events. Community is defined functionally, not spatially: it's a professional peer group rather than a neighborhood. Hired hands, from nannies to headmasters to therapists, bear more of the civic-virtue load than is typical.*[93]

Both my experience and that of Lemann's validated Robert Putnam's observations about the decline of civic engagement in America and held big cities accountable for the trend.

Based on my experience, here are several questions to ask ourselves when considering a geographic move: Are the people in this city like me, or do I want to be like them? Does the lifestyle match my current or desired lifestyle? If in-person work is important to you, can the location support your career? If you're single, will you be able to meet your ideal partner there?

Sadly, a significant number of people relocate to new places for incorrect reasons. One evening, my wife and I were at a dinner with another couple, and during our conversation, they mentioned that they wanted to move. Intrigued, we asked where they were considering relocating. Their response was, "Wherever there are low taxes and good sports access for the kids."

I was baffled by the idea that their decision-making criteria for such a significant life decision revolved around what

> **Sadly, a significant number of people relocate to new places for incorrect reasons.**

seemed to us like trivial things. *What about access to nature? Like-minded people?* It struck me as odd that they didn't seem to factor in the broader aspects of lifestyle and well-being that a new location could offer.

What role does your geography play in how you find belonging? How is it helping or hindering?

OVERALL HEALTH

Taking care of your physical, emotional, and mental well-being enables you to actively participate in the world around you. Staying healthy improves your capacity to engage in social activities and maintain relationships. This starts with your physical fitness, so you are not prohibited from participating in certain activities, and continues with your emotional health. We all need safe spaces to process the issues that life brings us so that we can be well-regulated, functioning adults.

> What role does your overall health play in how you find belonging? How is it helping or hindering?

RELATIONSHIP STATUS

The nature of your romantic life, whether you are single, dating, or in a committed relationship, determines, in part, the support network you have or lack. As I previously discussed, a healthy and secure relationship is arguably the single most important factor in fostering a sense of belonging.

Galloway, the NYU marketing professor, once stated that choosing a spouse is the single most important decision you'll make in your life. Not having one, he says, "makes the down times tougher and the upside less enjoyable."[94] To put it another way, a life partnership goes beyond the realms of romance and companionship and has a significant impact on our emotional well-being and overall happiness. Despite the scientifically proven benefits that marriage offers, it is surprising to note that one in four individuals is still unmarried at the age of forty.[95]

What role does your relationship status play in how you find belonging? How is it helping or hindering?

EDUCATION LEVEL

For my undergraduate education, I went to Hunter College, one of the schools within the City University of New York system. Despite its size of nearly twenty thousand students, it was a commuter school, so its campus was virtually non-existent—three boring buildings in the middle of Manhattan's Upper East Side. Like most of its students, I worked a full-time job throughout. The lack of a traditional college experience impacted how I perceived the school and, thus, how disengaged I was from its network.

Graduate school was a totally different experience for me. I went to business school at Georgetown University. The sprawling campus made it feel real, and the brand name made it feel important. Naturally I was much more attached to this experience, and thus more connected to its alumni network. Merely telling people I was a Georgetown grad—a Hoya—made people raise their eyebrows and approach me differently.

Education affects your social circles and inbound opportunities, impacting mostly your socioeconomic mobility. It also impacts your perception of where you think you belong. For example, if you perceive a situation to be "highbrow," you might subconsciously avoid it. It can even dictate the conversations you have, the people you meet, and the communities you feel comfortable in.

> What role does your education level play in how you find belonging? How is it helping or hindering?

EMPLOYMENT STABILITY

When I refer to employment stability, I'm referring to your job as a platform for finding belonging. This means that while your job itself won't contribute to your sense of belonging, its many "features"—potential friendships, recognition programs, affinity groups, industry event participation, and even dating opportunities—will.

Between 2011 and 2018, the company I founded, Social Tables, received nearly a dozen culture awards and recognitions. Taking culture seriously was a top priority for me as CEO. It would be a mistake if I didn't offer you some practical advice on finding a company with the right culture that matches your needs.

Begin by considering whether you are the type of person who enjoys a social workplace or if you prefer a more individualistic atmosphere. Don't assume that the cheesy team photos on the workplace's website guarantee

> **Don't assume that the cheesy team photos on the workplace's website guarantee a fun gig if you're looking for deeper connections.**

a fun gig if you're looking for deeper connections. Instead, make sure they cultivate a sense of community by organizing "extracurricular activities" like incentive trips, company outings, and voluntary after-work events.

Be advised—workplaces that strive to create a sense of community are not all fun and games. In fact, they may be overbearing, with high expectations from management to participate, engage in the culture, and "drink the Kool-Aid." I know because Social Tables was similar. I judged anyone who didn't attend an optional work happy hour or who didn't seem excited about our company's culture... and this was a terrible habit.

Many companies that recognize the need for workplace belonging try to create environments where employees feel like they are part of something bigger than themselves. The concept of "workism" suggests that work can provide a sense of community, meaning, and self-actualization, similar to the role organized religion has played throughout history.[96] Don't fall for this trap.

Having a stable job means more than just being employed: it involves feeling satisfied from and secure in your work. When you have these positive feelings, you are likely to build stronger relationships with your coworkers, feel appreciated, and receive recognition. These are the belonging fuels our workplace can provide. On the other hand, if you're unsatisfied with your job, you can feel isolated and anxious, which hinders your sense of belonging.

In *The Search*, Bruce Feiler offers valuable insights into finding the job that works for you. First, he says that you should be comfortable spending time in the periods of instability, because that's where your inner spirit will lead you to what's next. Second, he asks you to throw out the traditional notion that we're all "on a path," because our priorities change as life unfolds. Finally, he argues that the idea of a traditional job is no longer relevant, and we must reevaluate how we find fulfillment in our chosen endeavors.[97]

> What role does your employment play in how you find belonging? How is it helping or hindering?

SOCIOECONOMIC STATUS

Your socioeconomic status, which gauges your economic and social position, influences different parts of life, such as housing and education opportunities. Notably, this also influences the places where you spend your time. As journalist Katherine Hamilton observed in the *Wall Street Journal*, "more people are relying on gym memberships, art classes, and other paid activities to develop friendships," and these engagements are not cheap.[98]

> What role does your socioeconomic status play in how you find belonging? How is it helping or hindering?

CONSCIOUSNESS LEVEL

Imagine consciousness as a movie theater screen. Like how a screen brings images to life in a film, consciousness brings our experiences to life, capturing our thoughts, feelings, and sensations. The purpose of this screen is not to create the projections themselves but rather to provide a platform for us to perceive and participate in them. Consciousness is the state of being aware and able to think about one's existence and everything that comes with it.[99]

Various religions and philosophies have provided methods to understand consciousness throughout history. Some of these methods include Sufism's Seven Stations, Alcoholics Anonymous's 12 Steps, Zen Buddhism's Ten Oxherding Pictures, and David R. Hawkins's Map of Consciousness. Each of these spiritual maps helps individuals progress through different stages of personal and spiritual growth, leading them to a higher state of awareness, enlightenment, or union with the divine. In this book, we will use the Hawkins map.

> **Consciousness is the state of being aware and able to think about one's existence and everything that comes with it.**

Hawkins describes the levels of consciousness as a hierarchy of different states of being. At lower levels (below two hundred), such as Shame, Guilt, and Fear, behavior is driven by basic instincts, self-interest, and negative emotions.

As we move up the scale to levels like Courage, Accceptance, and Love, awareness expands. At these higher states (two hundred and above), life becomes more creative, harmonious, and interconnected. We show more love, compassion, and purpose.[100]

Each of these qualities makes us more open to and accepting of other people and experiences that come our way. It gives us wisdom to put our trust in something bigger than ourselves and the discernment to know right from wrong.

Higher consciousness is the difference between belonging that uplifts and belonging that restricts.

What role does your consciousness level play in how you find belonging? How is it helping or hindering?

Map of Consciousness[101]

700-1000	Enlightenment	Transcendence, Divine Inspiration, Ultimate Consciousness
600	Peace	God-consciousness, Synchronicity, Contribution
540	Joy	Unconditional Love, True Happiness, Positive Influence
500	Love	Reverence, Noble Intent, Universal Love
400	Reason	Rationality, Objectivity, Knowledge
350	Acceptance	Forgiveness, Harmony, Openness
310	Willingness	Optimism, Determination, Intention
250	Neutrality	Flexibility, Safety, Non-Judgment
200	Courage	Integrity, Confidence, Life Affirmation
175	Pride	Conditionality, Aggression, External Validation
150	Anger	Impatience, Desire, Frustration
125	Desire	Longing, Anxiety, Craving
100	Fear	Punishment, Separation, Regret
75	Grief	Loss, Hopelessness, Despair
50	Apathy	Despair, Giving Up, Indifference
30	Guilt	Blame, Wrongdoing, Self-Recrimination
20	Shame	Humiliation, Negation, Self-Hatred

↑
POWER
- -
FORCE
↓

EXERCISE *Complete this digitally at belongingquest.com/exercises*

FINDING YOUR CONSCIOUSNESS LEVEL

We will not rely on applied kinesiology or muscle testing like Hawkins did for measuring people's consciousness. Instead, I will offer three different methods for finding your consciousness level. I encourage you to use as many of these methods as you like. By using multiple methods and averaging the results, you can get a more balanced and precise assessment of your consciousness level.

Method 1: Trust your gut | Review the Map of Consciousness on the preceding page and the definitions for each level. What's your gut feeling about where you are? Trust it.

Method 2: Back into it | Review the table on the following page and select your view of life. The corresponding consciousness level is where you are.

Method 3: Phone a friend | Give a call to a friend who really knows you and won't hold back. Invite *them* to tell you what level they believe you are at. The people closest to you will likely know you the best.

Your environment plays a key role in providing the milieu for how you find belonging. If content (i.e., the ways in which you find belonging) is king, then context (i.e., your belonging environment) is God.

View of Life[102]

VIEW OF LIFE	ENERGETIC "FREQUENCY"	NAME OF LEVEL
Is	700-1000	Enlightenment
Perfect	600	Peace
Complete	540	Joy
Favorable	500	Love
Meaningful	400	Reason
Harmonious	350	Acceptance
Hopeful	310	Willingness
Satisfactory	250	Neutrality
Feasible	200	Courage
Demanding	175	Pride
Antagonistic	150	Anger
Disappointing	125	Desire
Frightening	100	Fear
Tragic	75	Grief
Hopeless	50	Apathy
Evil	30	Guilt
Miserable	20	Shame

Complete this digitally at belongingquest.com/exercises

EVALUATING YOUR ENVIRONMENT

Through evaluating and possibly changing certain aspects of our environment, we can profoundly improve or even reshape our sense of belonging. Positive disruptions, especially the ones we initiate, shake things up and make us reconsider how we achieve belonging. Though they may initially be unsettling, they can be a catalyst for personal or professional transformation.

Making changes, however, often presents a challenge, as people frequently fall victim to a status quo bias. They prefer stability and resist change, even if they acknowledge that making changes could lead to improved outcomes.

Moving to Boise was my way of rejecting the status quo trap. It was quite literally the opposite of not only what I planned to do—and what others expected me to do—but also of what I knew. I had never lived anywhere outside of the eastern standard time zone. Little did I know at the time, it was what I needed. It opened dozens of new doors for me.

To help prevent a status quo bias from happening to you, I suggest taking an inventory of your current environment using the table below.

1. In the first column, write out how the condition shows up in your life right now. As an example, we will use the geography row: "Apartment complex in downtown Miami."

2. In the second column, write out how it impacts your sense of belonging. "I get to enjoy the nightlife."
3. In the third column, write out how you want to address it. "Move closer to the water so I can enjoy nature."

Belonging Condition	How has the condition manifested in your life?	How does it impact your belonging?	What is one simple way you could address it?
Living Environment			
Cultural Identity			
Relationship Status			
Employment Stability			
Socioeconomic Status			
Overall Health			
Education Level			
Consciousness Level			

Don't aim to write a grand life plan in this exercise. It's a simple task to evaluate which present conditions are advantageous for you and which ones are not. Then, if you're so inclined, you can make changes to your life as you see fit.

Each of these belonging conditions also presents a crossroad moment—an opportunity to take a leap, expand your network, or try something new. As we grow older, crossroad moments start to wane. We settle into life's obligations as more people begin to rely on us and making changes becomes harder. For this reason, I urge you to consider acting on these desired changes sooner rather than later.

CHAPTER 11

THE COMPETENCIES AT THE TOP

*"No matter what your ability is, effort is what ignites
that ability and turns it into accomplishment."*
—CAROL S. DWECK

As I've grown older, I have gotten more comfortable with my sense of belonging. While I no longer have extended bouts of belonginglessness, I certainly do experience it from time to time. One of the more recent and prolonged experiences where I felt othered and isolated happened at a Group Relations Conference, or GRC.

A GRC is a structured event where participants explore and analyze group dynamics and behaviors in the present moment to gain insights into authority, roles, and relationships within groups. Another way to explain it is as a multiday meeting where people come together to learn about how they act and work with others by observing and discussing group interactions. Quite meta, I know.

The conference I attended, Leadership for Change, was organized by the University of San Diego's School of Leadership and Education Sciences. Arriving late to orientation allowed me to notice that I was one of three or four white men in a classroom of one hundred.

My demographic identity became even more pronounced during our small group breakout session. The room was arranged in a circle of chairs, and I immediately felt my unique position as the only straight white male in the group. Our group's consultant, John, assigned us the task of studying the "here and now." His job, I would soon learn, was to facilitate discussions by commenting on group dynamics he'd observe unfolding in real-time.

As a natural leader and a task-oriented person, I quickly tried to bring our group together to work on the task at hand.

"I see the white man is trying to take control," John said, staring blankly into the air.

What the actual fuck? I thought to myself. *Is this guy for real?*

I was met with resistance from virtually every one of my seven groupmates who preferred to shut me down rather than to get our job done. They shifted the conversation to small talk, which was followed by uncomfortable silence.

When I couldn't stand the lack of progress, I'd try to lead the group again.

"The white man is dominating the conversation," John said again, gazing into the ether. The group agreed with his incendiary feedback and accused me of a "negative tone" that was "not creating a safe space."

So much for teamwork, I thought. By the third group meeting I gave up and sat in silent resentment.

Apparently, this is exactly what's supposed to happen at a GRC. When the conference was over and John was out of the character he played, he told me that the way I showed up was exactly what our group needed.

In our small group, much like in the real world, we were dealing with issues of roles. People often unconsciously assign roles to others based on their identities, which reflects larger societal dynamics. As a white man, my presence brought up issues of power and privilege. Even though my "contributions" created tension and conflict, the group needed someone to represent these dynamics so they could confront and process their biases and behaviors.

Through this experience, I realized I am uncomfortable without control and direction, and I tend to play the victim to facilitate dependence. I learned that, instead of defensiveness, I should welcome vulnerability and curiosity. Most importantly, however, I learned that part of my work is fighting the

> Through this experience, I realized I am uncomfortable without control and direction, and I tend to play the victim to facilitate dependence.

deep and unconscious biases that influence how I show up to most of my interactions. All these maladaptive behaviors contributed to feeling like an outsider at the conference.

This experience of not feeling a sense of belonging at the GRC made me aware of the missing competencies that can hinder our sense belonging. My own skill gap led me to develop Belonging Intelligence, or Belonging IQ.

THE SKILLS OF BELONGING MASTERY

In contrast to emotional intelligence, or EQ, which covers a wide range of interpersonal skills that are an important baseline for navigating social situations, Belonging IQ hones in on the specific competencies that directly contribute to how we find and maintain connection with ourselves and with others.

> Belonging IQ hones in on the specific competencies that directly contribute to how we find and maintain connection with ourselves and with others.

Leveraging this "intelligence" is the key to not only *maintaining* but also *upgrading* your belonging archetype. It includes five skills: self-actualization, embracing risk, navigating rejection, cultivating social relationships, and exploring personal passions.

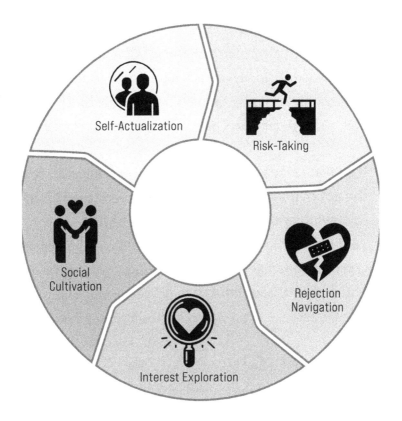

Self-Actualization

While self-awareness is about knowing yourself, *self-actualization* is about using that knowledge to keep growing and improving. It involves discovering and working toward your life's purpose, living in alignment with your values, and so much more.

You may not realize it, but self-actualization messages appear in pop culture all the time. The term "be your best self" is essentially a message to self-actualize. However, what these cliché slogans overlook is the fact that self-actualization is impossible without self-awareness. In other words, you can't be your best self if you don't know yourself to begin with!

If self-actualization is the act of constantly reviewing and updating your belonging fuel tank, you have been self-actualizing throughout The Quest. With every accomplished milestone and every completed exercise, you have been unearthing your potential.

> **If self-actualization is the act of constantly reviewing and updating your belonging fuel tank, you have been self-actualizing throughout The Quest.**

Additionally, incorporating your sense of belonging into your goal-planning system can help with self-actualization. For example, if you find belonging in crowds, you can commit to attending more of the gatherings that you enjoy as part of your next goal-setting exercise. If you prefer solitude, reading fiction with strong character development can help you establish symbolic bonds with the characters.

Incorporating belonging strategies that work well for you into your accountability practices is a guaranteed way to stay on the path of self-actualization. Surrendering to a path of self-actualization involves inherent risks. Welcoming them is the second skill we need to sharpen.

Risk-Taking

Risk-taking is a crucial part of personal growth. It involves everything from trying new belonging fuels to taking bold steps that change your belonging environment. After all, the most significant opportunities for lasting joy may lie outside your comfort zone.

Taking risks in terms of belonging means shaking up your social interactions and routines to avoid stagnation. It requires courage to explore new territory, like joining communities, talking to strangers, or reviving neglected interests. Bold moves like relocating, changing careers, or proposing to a life partner can also be forms of risk-taking.

This courage is crucial to finding belonging that aligns with your evolving self. Risk-taking is about actively shaping your social world, not passively accepting it. If the fear of failure is holding you back, take small steps like leaving a text group that brings you down or quitting a Facebook group that is filled with negativity. Before you realize it, you'll be attending concerts solo or publishing your fan fiction on the web.

> **Risk-taking is about actively shaping your social world, not passively accepting it.**

Taking on risks brings more rejection, so navigating rejection is our next competency.

Rejection Navigation

The ability to *navigate rejection* shows up in different ways when it comes to belonging. First, it's about the strength to drop something that doesn't serve you. To avoid the painful phrase "you don't belong here," we often hide our true selves and conform to the expectations of the groups we are a part of or the relationships we maintain, when instead we should just respectfully reject them.

> To avoid the painful phrase "you don't belong here," we often hide our true selves.

Another way rejection shows up is in our ability to manage it when we're staring it in the face. The truth of the matter is that rejection is a gift that gives us time back. If you continue to stay in a place where you don't fit in, you're only delaying the inevitable.

Here are four strategies to assist you in effectively dealing with rejection.

Detach from rejection. It's important to remember that if everyone always agrees with you, there's a chance you're doing something wrong. Prioritize meaningful connections that don't drain your energy as you maintain them.

Create a learning moment. Rather than seeing rejection as a personal failure, view it as an opportunity to gain insights about yourself and your interactions with others. Start by looking at the situation objectively. Reflect and consider the lessons to be learned. *Could you have communicated differently? Is there a relationship pattern that might contribute to these experiences?* Being objective helps you move beyond the emotional sting of rejection and toward constructive self-analysis.[103]

Listen for the truth. Even during the toughest moments, when rejection hurts deeply, there is usually a kernel of truth buried within this pain. Listen to it. Good listening requires effort to understand the other person's perspective. Think about how the person criticizing, even if they're being provocative, might have something meaningful to share. Better yet, listen with the notion that *they are right* and see what learnings await.[104]

Find peace in rejection. From a practical standpoint, it can be empowering to observe your emotions objectively. Recognize that while the feeling of rejection is valid, it won't last forever. It does not define you or your future relationships. Over time, its significance will diminish. I promise.

Managing rejection provides certain cover from inevitable social situations, but interest exploration opens new avenues for connection.

Interest Exploration

For me, one of the most thrilling aspects of the topic of belonging is that even if you've faced numerous setbacks, there is always a new path to discover. This is where *interest exploration* comes in.

Understanding that belonging can be experienced both in solitude and in social settings, I hold a strong belief in the value of independently exploring personal hobbies and interests. It's never too late to find something that genuinely energizes you. And the beautiful thing is that, for many of these things, you don't need anyone else.

Once you find something you love, you can build social habits around it. This can include making friends who share your interests, going on trips related to your hobby, and joining online groups.

Here is the process I used to find new hobbies. Start by making a list of things that bring you joy. Then, find as many hobbies as possible that contain items on this list. If something piques your interest, experiment to see if you can get into it.

Following this process I discovered reefkeeping. I love animals, technology, building things, and beautiful design. These four seemingly unrelated things led me to the hobby of maintaining saltwater aquariums. I enjoy caring for fish and coral, I leverage technology to maintain their habitat, and I design a beautiful ecosystem for them to flourish in.

I initially began with a freshwater setup, as it is simpler to maintain, and later transitioned to a saltwater setup. This hobby has led me to take scuba-diving trips, to participate in various online groups, and to hang out with other reefkeepers in my area.

As we find new interests, we meet new people, so we need a system to manage our growing connections.

Social Cultivation

Social cultivation is the practice of nurturing everything that helps you feel a sense of belonging—the check-ins with friends, phone calls to family, one-on-ones with colleagues, family meetings, and so on. This is often the work that gets us to belong.

According to research by Jeffrey A. Hall, a professor of communication studies, and director of the Relationships and Technology Lab at the University of Kansas, it usually takes around forty to sixty hours of quality time to go from being acquaintances to casual friends. From there, it takes approximately eighty to one hundred hours to transition from casual friends to close friends. Finally, to establish a close friendship, it takes over two hundred hours of shared experiences and interactions. However, it's not solely about the amount of time. It's the quality of the interactions that matter, and more meaningful interactions will speed up the process.[105]

This competency also requires a system for maintaining your relationships. You can utilize specialized customer relationship management (CRM) software like Clay or Relatable to manage personal relationships effectively. Or you can just take some time each week to go through your texts and catch up with friends. I find it helpful to have a list of friends in different cities I frequently visit, so I can easily get in touch with them when I'm there. Whatever works for you.

To help deepen our intimacy, Jen and I have actively participated in workshops and therapy for couples. It allows us to continually deepen our understanding of each other. To stay connected emotionally, we have a weekly check-in meeting on the calendar that includes a process for discussing difficult topics.

DEBRIEFING THE CLIMB

Just as I was wrapping up writing this book, I stumbled on an academic paper by psychologist Kelly-Ann Allen and colleagues entitled "Belonging: A Review of Conceptual Issues, an Integrative Framework, and Directions for Future Research."

As I read the words, "We also present an integrative framework on belonging and consider implications of this framework for future research and practice," my heart skipped a beat. What could they possibly be recommending that I hadn't seen?

I scrolled down to see what the *integrative framework* they were alluding to looked like. I paused to take it in. This team of esteemed researchers from around the world were proposing a set of tools like the one I had coalesced and developed for The Quest!

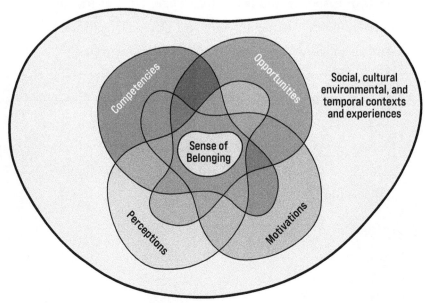

Their framework has five components, each of which neatly corresponds to the tools I have shared in The Quest:[106]

- **Motivations**. The inherent drive to form connections with others (belonging archetype).

- **Perceptions**. The thoughts and feelings about how we belong (belonging fuel tank).

- **Opportunities**. The chances that present themselves to find our sense of belonging (belonging fuels).

- **Competencies**. The skillset needed to connect and experience belonging (Belonging IQ).

- **Context**. As a dynamic social system, these four components mutually reinforce and influence each other across various contexts and experiences. This is the belonging environment.

Each of us has an innate desire to find belonging, but because we're all so different, we need an archetype to steer our *motivations* in the most effective direction. As we navigate life, we require a gauge like the belonging fuel tank to *perceive* how we're doing. Throughout our journey, we encounter different *opportunities* for belonging, which act as fuels for our tank. Each of these opportunities requires distinct *competencies* to negotiate, making our Belonging IQ a necessary toolkit by our side. The *context*, or belonging environment, in which we're operating needs to be regularly reevaluated to ensure we're thriving to our fullest potential.

POST-CLIMB REFLECTIONS

I imagine that as you've been going through The Quest you've experienced clarity about the subject of belonging for the first time. I have one more favor to ask of you.

Adopt a belonging mindset.

A mindset is simply the lens you use when making decisions. Using this mindset as life happens, choices need to be made, and opportunities present themselves will allow you to make decisions based on this new concept: belonging.

Adopt a belonging mindset.

Will this contribute to or dilute my sense of belonging?

The key message I want you to remember from this book is that there are no right or wrong ways to belong. It's what works for you. I hope that you not only vary your fuels but also continue to try out new ones.

Whatever paths you decide to take on this lifelong journey, may they bring you enduring joy, or may you possess the discernment to seek out other options. Just know that if and when you decide to return to The Quest, these pages will be here, ready to be your guiding light whenever you seek their wisdom.

A BRIEF GUIDE TO CREATING BELONGING

"People support what they help create."
—STEVEN R. COVEY

As the CEO of Social Tables, I may not have been perfect, but I succeeded in fostering an exceptionally unique culture of belonging. I have several metrics to back this up.

Despite being a small company with a peak of just one hundred employees, the company saw four marriages emerge from connections made there. Remarkably, over five years after the company's sale, former employee teams continue to follow each other to new companies, maintaining their professional relationships across different industries. Several friend groups that formed at Social Tables remain close to this day.

These enduring bonds are a testament to the effort my fellow *Tablers* put forth and are a source of personal pride for me that cannot be overstated.

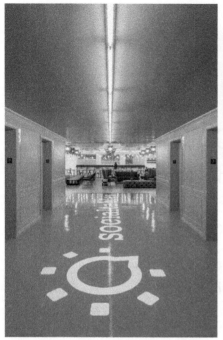

Left: The entryway to the Social Tables office in downtown Washington, DC

Above: On the left, a homage to the events industry with all the conference badges our employees had collected; and, on the right, a museum with memorablia from our company's history.

Unfortunately, the sense of belonging we had at Social Tables is not very common. The rise of hybrid workplaces, shifting generational values, and trite HR programs has made it even more challenging to create a sense of genuine belonging at work.

More challenging yet is the absence of an agreed-upon definition for belonging when it comes to the workplace. HR practitioners and consultants use the word *belonging* without being clear about its meaning. This is a crucial first step if we want this topic to become more legitimate.

From my experience, workplace belonging is an HR key performance indicator (KPI) that captures how well employees fit with and thrive within their environment. This fit includes employee-organization fit, employee-manager fit, and employee-team fit.

I purposely chose to assign the KPI to HR because calling it anything else would be disingenuous. Most belonging-related programs originate from HR, and like all HR initiatives, their aim is to drive employee performance and retention.

From my experience, workplace belonging is an HR key performance indicator (KPI) that captures how well employees fit with and thrive within their environment.

If HR leaders are serious about fostering a sense of belonging, they can begin by avoiding the Four Horsemen of the Workplace Apocalypse.

THE FOUR HORSEMEN OF THE WORKPLACE APOCALYPSE

Horseman #1: Conformity Pressure

In some workplaces, there is an unspoken expectation for employees to mold themselves to fit specific norms and behavior, often at the expense of their individuality. This conformity can lead to boring and uninspiring work environments.

An antidote to counteract this pressure is to promote individuality. Motivate staff members to bring their individual perspectives and personalities to discussions. While the city of

Austin keeps things weird, at Social Tables we avoided conformity via our "Be Outrageous" core value.

Horseman #2: Performance Neglect

Overemphasizing a belonging culture can sometimes lead to neglecting performance and accountability. Such an environment can foster leniency toward underperforming individuals, lower productivity, and increase resentment amongst staff.

The antidote is to uphold meritocracy. Remember, work is work. High performance must be rewarded and poor performance admonished. Ensure that everyone understands that belonging to the team also means maintaining high performance standards. Performance and culture must go together.

Horseman #3: Inclusion Illusion

While many workplaces say they value inclusion, they only seem to prefer people who share a similar ideology or have similar characteristics. This can alienate those who don't fit this mold and stifle true inclusivity.

The antidote is *actual* inclusion. True inclusion means creating an environment that embraces a wide range of personality types, working styles, and viewpoints. It should not compromise performance.

Horseman #4: Dependency Culture

When employees rely too much on their employer to fill their sense of belonging, they become dependents. This leads to fruitless attempts at appeasement (e.g., more snacks, more PTO, and so on).

The antidote is to promote autonomy. Encourage employees to develop a sense of belonging outside of work first. Provide the space and resources for them to pursue personal interests and build networks beyond the workplace. This not only fosters independence but also brings diverse experiences and perspectives back into the workplace.

> **Encourage employees to develop a sense of belonging outside of work first.**

HOW TO CREATE A SENSE OF BELONGING ON TEAMS

A *culture of belonging* refers to an organizational environment where employees feel deeply connected to their company or team. In such a culture, employees can show up authentically, are recognized for their contributions, and clearly see how they fit into the larger picture.

Before we proceed, I'd like to offer a word of caution. Cultivating a culture of belonging is not for every leader or leadership team. It requires a significant commitment and effort far beyond what

> **In such a culture, employees can show up authentically, are recognized for their contributions, and clearly see how they fit into the larger picture.**

is needed for a typical organizational culture. You should be fully aware of the dedication this entails before moving forward.

In fact, if I were starting Social Tables 2.0 today, I'm not certain that I'd implement a belonging culture. The business benefits, such as higher performance, don't always outweigh the challenges, which can include a sense of entitlement among some employees and increased budgetary demands. This perspective comes with success under my belt; I wouldn't have the same pressure to drive performance the second time around.

If I were going back in time to *truly* do it all over again, then I have no doubt that I would implement a culture of belonging.

The Critical Path to a Culture of Belonging

Whether you're thinking about belonging at the team level or taking an organizational approach, creating a culture of belonging will directly correlate with high performance. Here are the five steps to developing such a culture:

1. **Hospitality.** Belonging starts with hospitality. This can be achieved through a warm environment, a comfortable setting, and sincere greetings, especially from leaders. This sets the tone for the team's culture. The idea that hospitality is a pleasure—that it feels great to treat teammates with warmth, care, and kindness—needs to be ingrained into the culture.[107]

	FEELINGS	BEHAVIORS	OUTCOMES
HOSPITALITY	"I feel welcome." / "People are genuine."	Warmth in the way people interact / The experience is not overwhelming	Peer recognition
SAFETY	"I feel safe." / "I can be myself." / "I don't feel judged."	Members are open and vulnerable / Members respect and trust each other	Diversity metrics
ENGAGEMENT	"I am eagerly participating." / "I am learning from teammates."	Members cross-pollinate beyond immediate circles / Members participate and contribute	Engagement scores / Participation rate
COMMITMENT	"I prioritize this team." / "I am committed to our success."	Member retention is high / Members refer other members and ensure they succeed	Retention / Referrals
BELONGING	"I belong here." / "You belong here."	Members proudly identify with the community / Members advocate for the community	Individual performance / Workplace satisfaction

2. **Safety**. Establishing a psychologically safe environment guarantees that all team members can freely express themselves without worrying about criticism or negative consequences. It fosters trust, encourages mutual respect, and promotes vulnerability. At Social Tables, we began each executive team meeting with the following preamble:

   Great teams do not hold back from one another. They are unafraid to engage in open and constructive conflict. They admit to their mistakes, their weaknesses, and their concerns without fear of reprisal. They hold each team member accountable and ensure a high standard of performance.

3. **Engagement**. Once team members feel safe, they start to collaborate, engage actively, and openly share their ideas. They actively listen and eagerly participate because their fears of rejection have been alleviated.

4. **Commitment**. Engagement that fulfills individuals both personally and professionally leads to increased commitment on the team. As commitment increases, members begin to prioritize each other, and with that, the team itself. Employee retention increases.

5. **Belonging**. Finally, a feeling of belonging emerges as everyone recognizes and appreciates each other's contributions and sees each other's dedication. No one's fit is questioned, the team is in harmony, and workplace satisfaction rises.

Ownership and Transparency to Drive Results

There are two items that I consider table stakes when it comes to ensuring a culture of belonging sticks: ownership and transparency. The first gets our virtuous cycle going while the second maintains it.

Ownership, in our sense of the word, is radical inclusion. It is an absolute necessity when it comes to creating a culture of belonging because it sets the tone to set the tone. By involving *all* colleagues in the development of a company's building blocks, such as core values, mission statement, and vision statement, we level up an organization's sense of belonging overnight.

> **Ownership, in our sense of the word, is radical inclusion.**

When I first started Social Tables, I gathered our five-person team—including the intern—in a small conference room. We went around the table as everyone shared the values that mattered most to them. We jotted their ideas on the whiteboard. The few patterns that emerged became our first set of core values:[108]

- "~~No because~~ Yes if" to embody our can-do attitude.

- "High risk, high reward" to explain why we're committed to the start-up journey.

- "Ship all day, party all night" to reflect both our work ethic and camaraderie.

- "Fail fast and often" to capture our iterative mindset

Over the next eighteen months, our company grew to around twenty people, and we replicated the exercise with even greater enthusiasm. I cordoned off a room for an entire workday for this special event. Each employee was given a stack of Post-its and was asked to write down the values they believed we currently possess or the values that they'd like us to nurture. They were instructed to place the stickies on the walls of the meeting room. By the end of the day, the walls were adorned with more than one hundred Post-its. We then took this physical word cloud and combined comparable words—resulting in the second iteration of our values.[109]

About a year and a half later, when we had reached the one-hundred-employee milestone, I continued this tradition. I established a diverse, employee-only committee and tasked them with reviewing our values and proposing any changes. They exceeded expectations by phasing out certain values, keeping others, and introducing a handful of new ones.

My experience in developing core values through crowd-sourcing and open-sourcing incomplete vision statements has taught me that committed employees will devise company artifacts that are superior to anything the leadership team could conceive of on their own.

> **Once a belonging culture is established, it's the leader's job to maintain it.**

Once a belonging culture is established, it's the leader's job to maintain it. A surefire way to do so is to be transparent about the company's performance, challenges, and opportunities early and often. At Social Tables, we started having monthly company-wide meetings very early on and continued that tradition until the day we sold. At every single meeting I would review major KPIs—from monthly sales numbers to cash-on-hand.

But my sharing didn't stop there. We distributed sanitized versions of our monthly memos to the board along with slide decks from its quarterly meetings. By including employees in all the issues that the company deals with, employees feel included and valued.[110]

BELONGING DOES NOT BELONG IN DEI

The expansion of diversity, equity, and inclusion (DEI) programs to include belonging marked a significant shift in the conversation around workplace culture. Initially, I viewed this evolution as a positive step, signaling a deeper recognition of the need for emotional and psychological inclusion alongside traditional diversity and inclusion programs. I even created a meme to explain the difference among these terms.

DIVERSITY
Being invited
to the party

INCLUSION
Being asked to
dance at the party

BELONGING
Being comfortable
to dance as you are

The intention behind this meme is to illustrate that diversity is achieved by involving people from different backgrounds, inclusion is achieved when everyone participates (and yes, at the workplace everyone *must* participate), and belonging is achieved when everyone can participate in a way that is genuine to them.

However, as I further explored the subject, I became increasingly uneasy about categorizing belonging under the DEI umbrella. It took me a while, but I finally uncovered the root cause of my discomfort. The reason belonging doesn't "belong" with DEI is because, unlike the objective nature of DEI, belonging is a subjective outcome that depends on each individual's feelings, experiences, and sense of belonging.

A CEO can ask their team to boost the number of women in senior roles by 50 percent in the next three quarters, but they can't guarantee that every employee will feel included.

Belonging becomes even messier when you consider all the dynamics that can impact it, some of which have nothing to do with the workplace itself! How can we set belonging objectives when we can't fully influence their outcome?

> **Unlike the objective nature of DEI, belonging is a subjective outcome that depends on each individual's feelings, experiences, and sense of belonging.**

I have come to realize that when HR professionals and thought leaders use the word *belonging*, they are simply using it as a synonym for diversity.

Look no further than Stanford University professor Geoffrey L. Cohen's book, *Belonging: The Science of Creating Connection and Bridging Divides.* In his chapter dedicated to belonging at work, Cohen cites over two dozen workplace-related studies that, he says, highlight the employers' failure to create a sense of belonging.

Whether he is sharing data to show that the wage gap is alive and well, that work from home creates inequity, that employment tests are discriminatory, or that hiring managers continue to operate with an unconscious bias, he systematically makes the case that more DEI is the answer to achieving belonging in the workplace.

While all the issues he raises are both important and legitimate, they in fact have nothing to do with workplace belonging, which I have defined as a sense of fit between employees and the organization. By spreading misinformation, Cohen and other DEI practitioners have contributed to four common belonging mythologies:

Myth #1: "Belonging Can Be Standardized"

This notion fails to consider the personal and emotional nature of belonging, which organizational strategies cannot mandate or fully control. Unlike DEI, where specific initiatives can have an impact, no matter how much time or money is spent on a belonging initiative, it will never be enough. This is because it's an inherently subjective experience.

In fact, optimizing the workplace for the type of people who find belonging in the workplace directly opposes diversity efforts. If an organization tailors its environment to suit the needs of those who already feel a sense of belonging, it may inadvertently exclude other people.

Myth #2: "Belonging Is Solely the Organization's Responsibility"

Unlike DEI, belonging is the responsibility of both employer and employee. It takes two to tango because, again, belonging is about fit. Belonging requires active participation from the workforce. You can't simply tell employees they belong and expect it to just happen. Similarly, no matter how hard they try, employees cannot have belonging without the help and buy-in of their employer. For instance, if an employee wants to bring their teammates together but the company discourages such behavior, the employee's efforts are essentially worthless.

Myth #3: "Exclusion Is Bad"

Contrary to popular belief, exclusion is not inherently bad. *Conscious exclusivity*—the intentional practice of excluding certain individuals who don't share the same values—is a great way to uphold a culture's integrity. The truth is that not everyone belongs everywhere, and this is especially true in a high performing environment.

Myth #4: "DEI Is Morally Just"

While working toward a more diverse, equitable, and inclusive workplace is an exceptionally ethical goal—one that will never be "done"—it may in some instances ignore actual differences between people that organizations need to filter for. For example, a DEI program may focus on achieving gender diversity in an industry where the proportion of men and women is inherently unequal. Similarly, certain job roles may require physical or emotional capabilities that are more prevalent in one gender than the other. DEI initiatives must be grounded in common sense; they cannot ignore our biological differences. Recognizing these differences ensures that all individuals are supported in ways that acknowledge their unique needs and strengths, leading to a truly inclusive and effective workplace.

> **Recognizing these differences ensures that all individuals are supported in ways that acknowledge their unique needs and strengths, leading to a truly inclusive and effective workplace.**

INTEGRATING BELONGING INTO ORGANIZATIONS

Let's delve into the practical application of the belonging fuels that were introduced in The Quest. These fuels are just as useful to teams as they are to individuals.

 Interpersonal Relationships

The interpersonal relationships fuel centers on the importance of close friends. Research by Gallup has taught us that employees who have strong friendships at work are more engaged, productive, and loyal.[111]

The workplace can be a powerful platform for employees when it comes to building these meaningful relationships. Therefore, encouraging employees to form bonds helps create a cohesive work environment. And it's good for retention too.

At Social Tables, we did several things to help employees connect. Employees were asked to wear magnetic nametags—as opposed to cheap stickers—at company events. This prevented any awkwardness for team members who weren't good with names. An additional benefit of this cultural norm was that it increased intermingling because we found that simply not remembering someone's name was a reason to not approach them.

Additionally, we gave mentors who signed up to help onboard new employees gift certificates to the local coffee shop, so their coffee hangs were on us. And on many days, I personally ensured no one sat alone at lunch.

Collective Experiences

The collective experiences path can be used to foster a sense of belonging through company events and meetings. These gatherings can be powerful moments of connection, where employees feel part of something bigger than themselves. They create a space for employees to unite, celebrate successes, and feel a sense of camaraderie. It's where they can realize how much their work matters.

Do consider different belonging archetypes when planning your programs. That means creating inclusive events for team members that don't necessarily have a high NTBS score. Not everyone will feel comfortable attending every company function, and that's okay. Attendance at social events should never be punitive. Instead, offer various opportunities for connection that cater to different personalities and preferences.

Corporate experiences don't have to be company-wide or social in nature. Retreats and offsites are important tools not just for planning for the quarter or designing a major sprint. They foster a sense of belonging on the team. These small meetings are especially important for senior teams at the board, executive, and management levels.

Remember to include different activity types outside of meals and official business to connect with one another at a more personal level. Spending two or more days together, even with some of the messiness that comes from it, is important to getting everyone on the same team.

> Retreats and offsites are important tools not just for planning for the quarter or designing a major sprint. They foster a sense of belonging on the team.

Throughout my years in the hospitality industry, nothing has given me more joy than seeing a team come together to achieve great things. There's a magic that happens when we form, norm, and storm. Unfortunately, the group-travel segment of the industry has not caught up with the increasing demand for small meetings. Hotels and visitor bureaus are busy chasing large events and conferences, often ignoring the legitimate needs of smaller teams. This is why I started my new company, Assemble Hospitality Group.

Assemble is a new lodging concept offering purpose-built, exclusive-use venues in smaller markets for multi-day offsites and retreats. We provide a concierge service that plans every last detail, allowing teams to focus on having successful meetings rather than worrying about logistics like who is ordering pizza. Our first location is in Boise, Idaho and will open in the first quarter of 2025.

At a company level, Social Tables had an annual internal industry education event called "ST Conf" for all our employees. Everyone got the day off and attended educational talks led by their peers. These large-scale events can boost morale and foster a sense of belonging. We also had weekly happy hours where, once a month, we did not serve alcoholic beverages.

Casual Encounters

Casual encounters are the chance encounters that regularly happen all around us. Creating more opportunities for such "collisions" in your work environment can benefit those who thrive on unexpected interactions. They tend to take place more often in open-floor plans, hallways, break rooms, or during work breaks. The deliberate design of spaces, whether in the physical or virtual realm, that fosters impromptu conversations can greatly contribute to a sense of belonging.[112]

Incorporate areas where employees can casually interact without the pressure of formal meetings. These spaces should be inviting and strategically placed to maximize microinteractions. Valuing these informal interactions will contribute to the employees' sense of belonging.

At Social Tables, we encouraged employees to follow the Walmart ten-foot rule: we urged them to greet any colleague that was within ten feet of them. Employees lived our love for hospitality by acting as brand ambassadors when they saw a visitor walk off the elevator.

> **Valuing these informal interactions will contribute to the employees' sense of belonging.**

 ## Symbolic Bonds

The symbolic bonds path comes in many flavors, but the one we're concerned with is the one-sided relationship fuel. While it may not be feasible for leaders to have personal connections with every employee, they can still be accessible and approachable. Leaders who share personal insights, stories, or challenges help demystify the hierarchical gap that exists between them and the line. This makes them more relatable and makes employees more committed.

Q&A sessions, video messages, open DMs, anonymous surveys, and so on can serve as platforms for leaders to engage with employees, even at larger companies. Being open and willing to listen not only builds trust but also shows that everyone is valued.

At Social Tables, my calendar was open for anyone who wanted to schedule a meeting. I took questions and feedback—anonymous and not—during our monthly all-hands meetings and via weekly Q&As, virtual ask-me-anythings (AMAs,) and regular employee pulse surveys. In fact, I was part of the bullpen and did not have an office for our first six years.

Esteem-Building

Recognizing and validating employees is essential for fostering a sense of belonging. Some people need acknowledgment and praise more than others to feel connected and valued. Therefore, it's important to incorporate award programs that celebrate individual and team achievements. These can range from a President's Circle program to formal awards ceremonies to informal shout-outs in team meetings.

At Social Tables, we integrated awards into our monthly company meetings. Additionally, we organized a yearly company award ceremony named The Chiavaris, where we recognized outstanding employees by presenting awards and superlatives, including the highly sought-after Golden Chiavari for "Tabler of the Year."

Thanks for letting me share this bonus chapter with you. Building a high-performance team is a lofty goal in and of itself. Crafting a culture of belonging to go along with it is next level. I commend you for focusing on it.

BETA SHEET

In climbing, a beta sheet is the set of instructions to climb a particular route. If you are a structured person, consider this a cheat sheet for the process I laid out in this book.

1. Create your initial belonging fuel tank to see how you currently find belonging.

2. Identify your belonging archetype: Eager Chimp, Anxious Meerkat, Reluctant Snow Leopard, or Independent Wolf.

3. Align your belonging fuel tank with your belonging archetype.

4. Use the Five C's to create the ideal version of your belonging fuel tank; the goal is to experience a life with more joy.

5. Evaluate your environment to see how it may restrict your sense of belonging. Make any necessary changes.

6. Integrate the competencies of Belonging IQ to stay at the summit of belonging.

MOUNTAIN LINGO

Attachment Style: The characteristic way in which individuals form emotional bonds and interact with others, shaped by early relationships and experiences.

Belonging: The sense of fit within a social system where an individual feels accepted and essential, while experiencing moments that reinforce these feelings.

Belonging Archetype: A unique archetype, consisting of one's attachment style and NTBS score, that defines how an individual seeks and experiences belonging. Archetypes include eager belonging, anxious belonging, reluctant belonging, and independent belonging.

Belonging (at work): An HR KPI that captures how well employees fit with and thrive within their environment

Belonging Crisis: America's epidemic of isolation and loneliness.

Belonging Environment: The various stable and semi-stable circumstances in our lives that can either constrict or expand the belonging opportunities that come our way. These include cultural identity, geography, overall health, relationship status, education level, employment stability, socioeconomic status, and consciousness level.

Belonging Fuel: The six paths that help each of us feel a sense of belonging—interpersonal relationships, collective experiences, casual encounters, symbol bonds, esteem-building, and contemplative practices.

Belonging Fuel Tank: The metaphorical reservoir of an individual's sense of belonging, which can be filled or depleted based on their social interactions and experiences. Any emptiness in the tank represents loneliness.

Belonging IQ: The collection of competencies needed to find and sharpen one's sense of belonging. Self-actualization, risk-taking, rejection navigation, social cultivation, and interest exploration.

Belonging Mindset: A mindset that considers challenges and opportunities through a belonging lens.

Belonging Subfuel. A secondary fuel within a Belonging Fuel.

Need to Belong Scale (NTBS): A psychological instrument that measures our fundamental human drive to form and maintain strong, stable, interpersonal relationships.

ACKNOWLEDGEMENTS

First and foremost, to my wife, Jen, who cheered me on every step of the way—from the first word to the last—thank you. She proofread sentences and reviewed images more times than I care to admit. And not once, throughout this often painstaking process, did she say no. I love you so much.

This book has been a three-year process, and I'm especially grateful to Evan Schnittman who coached me along the way. Thanks also to those who helped me with words: Erin, Chip, Ezra, and Michael.

I'd like to thank those I interviewed for this book: Scott Galloway, Robert Waldinger, Paul Stamets, Brad Mosell, and Brom Rector. I'd also like to thank my beta readers, Roni Berger, Matt Cohen, Trevor Lynn, and Nathan Huey.

Finally, I'd like to share my deep appreciation for the countless researchers, writers, and scholars whose shoulders I stand on with this book. Thank you for your contributions to your respective fields. They have enabled me to do my part.

DAN BERGER
Boise, Idaho
July 2024

WORKS CITED

Arendt, Hannah. *The Origins of Totalitarianism* (New York: Harcourt, Brace & Co., 1951).

Bolles, Richard N. *The Search: The How to Land Your Dream Job in the Digital World* (Berkeley: Ten Speed Press, 2022).

Buford, Bob. *Halftime: Moving from Success to Significance* (Grand Rapids: Zondervan, 1994).

Gilbert, Elizabeth. *Eat, Pray, Love: One Woman's Search for Everything Across Italy, India and Indonesia* (New York: Viking, 2006).

Gray, Nick. *The 2-Hour Cocktail Party: How to Build Big Relationships with Small Gatherings* (New York: Independently published, 2022).

Mounk, Yascha. *The Identity Trap: A Story of Ideas and Power in Our Time* (New York: Penguin Press, 2022).

Tatkin, Stan. *Wired for Love: How Understanding Your Partner's Brain and Attachment Style Can Help You Defuse Conflict and Build a Secure Relationship* (Oakland: New Harbinger Publications, 2012).

Tolle, Eckhart. *The Power of Now: A Guide to Spiritual Enlightenment* (Novato: New World Library, 1999).

ENDNOTES

1 Nancy Newton Verrier, *The Primal Wound: Understanding the Adopted Child* (Baltimore: Gateway Press, 1993).

2 "Belonging" in *Oxford Advanced Learner's Dictionary*, Oxford University Press, https://www.oxfordlearnersdictionaries.com/us/definition/english/belonging?q=belonging.

3 Abraham H. Maslow, "Maslow's Hierarchy of Needs," *Psychological Review* 50, no. 4 (1943).

4 Abraham H. Maslow, "A Theory of Human Motivation," *Psychological Review* 50, no. 4 (1943): 370–396.

5 Douglas T. Kenrick, Vladas Griskevicius, Steven L. Neuberg, and Mark Schaller, "Renovating the Pyramid of Needs: Contemporary Extensions Built Upon Ancient Foundations," *Perspectives on Psychological Science* 5, no. 3 (2010): 292–314, https://doi.org/10.1177/1745691610369469.

6 Douglas T. Kenrick et al., "An Updated Hierarchy of Fundamental Human Motives," *Perspectives on Psychological Science* 5, no. 3 (2010), https://doi.org/10.1177/1745691610369469.

7 Santokh S. Anant, "The Need to Belong," *Canada's Mental Health* 14, no. 2 (1966): 21–27.

8 Bonnie M. Hagerty and Kathleen L. Patusky, "Developing a Measure of Sense of Belonging," *Nursing Research* 44, no. 1 (1995): 9–13.

9   Roy F. Baumeister and Mark R. Leary, "The Need to Belong: Desire for Interpersonal Attachments as a Fundamental Human Motivation," *Psychological Bulletin* 117, no. 3 (1995): 497–529.

10 Nathaniel M. Lambert et al., "To Belong Is to Matter: Sense of Belonging Enhances Meaning in Life," *Journal of Personality and Social Psychology* 104, no. 2 (2013): 301–317.

11 Kelly-Ann Allen, Margaret L. Kern, Christopher S. Rozek, Dennis McInerney, and George M. Slavich, "Belonging: A Review of Conceptual Issues, an Integrative Framework, and Directions for Future Research," *Australian Journal of Psychology* 73, no. 1 (2021): 87–102, https://doi.org/10.1080/00049530.2021.1883409.

12 Ibid.

13 Susie Wise, *Design for Belonging: How to Build Inclusion and Collaboration in Your Communities* (Stanford, CA: Stanford University Press, 2022), 7.

14 Brené Brown, *The Gifts of Imperfection* (Center City, MN: Hazelden Information & Educational Services, 2010).

15 Brené Brown, *Braving the Wilderness: The Quest for True Belonging and the Courage to Stand Alone* (New York: Random House, 2017).

16 Ibid.

17 John Welwood, *Toward a Psychology of Awakening: Buddhism, Psychotherapy, and the Path of Personal and Spiritual Transformation* (Boston: Shambhala Publications, 2000).

18 Robert Putnam, *The Upswing: How America Came Together a Century Ago and How We Can Do It Again* (New York: Simon & Schuster, 2020).

19 The Cigna Group, "Loneliness Epidemic Persists: A Post-Pandemic Look," accessed June 17, 2024, https://newsroom.thecignagroup.com/loneliness-epidemic-persists-post-pandemic-look.

20 Linda M. Richmond, "Surgeon General Calls for Action to Address Youth Mental Health Crisis," *Psychiatric News* 57, no. 2 (2022), https://psychnews.psychiatryonline.org/doi/10.1176/appi.pn.2022.2.11.

21 US Department of Health and Human Services, "New Surgeon General Advisory Raises Alarm about the Devastating Impact of the Epidemic of Loneliness and Isolation in the United States," last modified May 3, 2023, https://www.hhs.gov/about/news/2023/05/03/new-surgeon-general-advisory-raises-alarm-about-devastating-impact-epidemic-loneliness-isolation-united-states.html.

22 Richard V. Reeves, "American Men Are Dying Younger," Of Boys and Men, December 15, 2023, https://ofboysandmen.substack.com/p/american-men-are-dying-younger.

23 Richard V. Reeves, "The Fragile Beauty of Male Friendship," Of Boys and Men, April 1, 2023, https://ofboysandmen.substack.com/p/the-fragile-beauty-of-male-friendship.

24 Jamie Ducharme, "COVID-19 Is Making America's Loneliness Epidemic Even Worse," *Time*, May 8, 2020, https://time.com/5833681/loneliness-covid-19/.

25 Douglas Belkin, "They Entered College in Isolation and Leave among Protests: The Class That Missed Out on Fun," *Wall Street Journal*, accessed May 4, 2024, https://www.wsj.com/us-news/education/college-fun-covid-pandemic-anxiety-ea992cee.

26 The Cigna Group, "Loneliness and the Workplace: 2020 US Report," https://legacy.cigna.com/static/www-cigna-com/docs/about-us/newsroom/studies-and-reports/combatting-loneliness/cigna-2020-loneliness-report.pdf.

27 Lydia Anderson, Chanell Washington, Rose M. Kreider, and Thomas Gryn, "Share of One-Person Households More Than Tripled from 1940 to 2020," United States Census Bureau, June 8, 2023, https://

www.census.gov/library/stories/2023/06/more-than-a-quarter-all-households-have-one-person.html.

28   US Census Bureau, 1940–90 Census, 2000 Census Summary File 2, 2010 Census Summary File 1, 2020 Decennial Censuses Demographic and Housing Characteristics File (DHC), "More Americans Are Living Alone," June 8, 2023, https://www.census.gov/library/stories/2023/06/more-than-a-quarter-all-households-have-one-person.html.

29   John T. Cacioppo and William Patrick, *Loneliness: Human Nature and the Need for Social Connection* (New York: WW Norton & Company, 2008), 7.

30   Robert Putnam, *The Upswing: How America Came Together a Century Ago and How We Can Do It Again* (New York: Simon & Schuster, 2020), 112.

31   Ibid.

32   "Pete Buttigieg Discusses America's Crisis of Belonging," *New Yorker*, October 14, 2019, video, https://www.newyorker.com/video/watch/the-new-yorker-festival-pete-buttigieg.

33   Ibid.

34   David Brooks, *The Second Mountain: The Quest for a Moral Life* (New York: Random House, 2019).

35   "Anne Applebaum on What Liberals Misunderstand about Authoritarianism," May 17, 2022 in *The Ezra Klein Show*, Apple Podcasts: Society & Culture, accessed February 2, 2024, https://podcasts.apple.com/ca/podcast/anne-applebaum-on-what-liberals-misunderstand-about/id1548604447.

36   Chavie Lieber, "Can You Solve Loneliness? These Start-Ups Are Betting on It," *Wall Street Journal* magazine, February 20, 2024, accessed June 7, 2024, https://www.wsj.com/health/wellness/loneliness-epidemic-belong-centers-daybreaker-34a8eb90.

37   Steve Leder, "Don't Wait to Live," interview by Elise Loehnen, Elise Loehnen, accessed March 13, 2023, https://www.eliseloehnen.com/episodes/rabbi-steve-leder-dont-wait-to-live.

38   Ram Dass, *Be Here Now* (New York: Harmony, 1971), 56.

39   Jonathan Haidt, *The Happiness Hypothesis: Finding Modern Truth in Ancient Wisdom* (New York: Basic Books, 2006), 239.

40   Steven Pinker, *The Blank Slate: The Modern Denial of Human Nature* (New York: Viking, 2002), 50.

41   Sonja Lyubomirsky, Kennon M. Sheldon, and David Schkade, "Pursuing Happiness: The Architecture of Sustainable Change," *Review of General Psychology* 9, no. 2 (2005): 111–131.

42   Phil Stutz and Barry Michels, *The Tools: 5 Tools to Help You Find Courage, Creativity, and Willpower—and Inspire You to Live Life in Forward Motion* (New York: Spiegel & Grau, 2012).

43   Ibid.

44   Elaine Paravati, Esha Naidu, and Shira Gabriel, "From 'Love Actually' to Love, Actually: The Sociometer Takes Every Kind of Fuel," *Self and Identity* 20, no. 1 (2020): 6–24, https://doi.org/10.1080/15298868.2020.1743750.

45   Jennifer L. Hirsch and Margaret S. Clark, "Multiple Paths to Belonging That We Should Study Together," *Perspectives on Psychological Science* 14, no. 2 (2019): 238–255, https://doi.org/10.1177/1745691618803629.

46   Elaine Paravati, Esha Naidu, and Shira Gabriel, "From 'Love Actually' to Love, Actually: The Sociometer Takes Every Kind of Fuel," *Self and Identity* 20, no. 1 (2020): 6–24, https://doi.org/10.1080/15298868.2020.1743750.

47   Ibid.

48   Mary Anne Dunkin, "Myths and Facts about Antidepressant Side-Effects," WebMD, July 20, 2023, https://www.webmd.com/depression/fears-and-facts-about-antidepressants.

49   Britta K. Hölzel, James Carmody, Mark Vangel, Christina Congleton, Sita M. Yerramsetti, Tim Gard, and Sara W. Lazar, "Mindfulness Practice Leads to Increases in Regional Brain Gray Matter Density," *Psychiatry Research: Neuroimaging* 191, no. 1 (2011): 36–43, doi:10.1016/j.pscychresns.2010.08.006.

50   Roy F. Baumeister and Mark R. Leary, "The Need to Belong: Desire for Interpersonal Attachments as a Fundamental Human Motivation," *Psychological Bulletin* 117, no. 3 (1995): 497–529; Mark R. Leary and Shira Gabriel, "The Relentless Pursuit of Acceptance and Belonging," *Advances in Motivational Science* 9 (2022): 135–178; Mark R. Leary et al., "Construct Validity of the Need to Belong Scale: Mapping the Nomological Network," *Journal of Personality and Social Psychology* 92, no. 5 (2007): 1028–1041.

51   Mark R. Leary, Kristine M. Kelly, Catherine A. Cottrell, and Lisa S. Schreindorfer, "Construct Validity of the Need to Belong Scale: Mapping the Nomological Network," *Journal of Personality Assessment* 95, no. 6 (2013): 610–624. Slightly modified for print.

52   Patrik Lindenfors, Andreas Wartel, and Johan Lind, "'Dunbar's Number' Deconstructed," *Biology Letters* 17 (May 2021), https://doi.org/10.1098/rsbl.2021.0158.

53   Susan Spreecher, "Social Bonding in Initial Acquaintance: Effects of Modality and Modality Order," *Social Psychology Quarterly* 84, no. 3 (September 2021): 216–234, https://doi.org/10.1177/01902725211030252.

54   Douglas T. Kenrick, Vladas Griskevicius, Steven L. Neuberg, and Mark Schaller, "Renovating the Pyramid of Needs: Contemporary Extensions Built upon Ancient Foundations," *Perspectives on Psychological Science* 5, no. 3 (2010): 292–314, https://doi.org/10.1177/1745691610369469.

55   Paul J. Dunion, "The Difference between Episodic Intimacy and Committed Intimacy," Psychology Today, July 6, 2024, https://www.psychologytoday.com/us/blog/the-secular-mystic-path/202407/episodic-intimacy-vs-committed-intimacy.

56   Scott Galloway, interview by author, Boise, ID, March 8, 2022.

57   Olga Khazan, "Stop Firing Your Friends: Just Make More of Them," *Atlantic*, June 28, 2023, https://www.theatlantic.com/ideas/archive/2023/06/stop-breaking-up-with-friends/674540/.

58   Ibid.

59   David R. Hawkins, *Power versus Force: The Hidden Determinants of Human Behavior* (Carlsbad, CA: Hay House, 2002).

60   Robert Waldinger, *The Good Life: Lessons from the World's Longest Scientific Study of Happiness* (New York: Simon & Schuster, 2021), 29.

61   Robert Waldinger, interview by author, Boise, ID, March 7, 2024.

62   David W. McMillan and David M. Chavis, "Sense of Community: A Definition and Theory," *Journal of Community Psychology* 14, no. 1 (1986): 6–23.

63   Ibid.

64   Richard Millington, "Different Types of Communities," FeverBee, November 23, 2010, accessed February 8, 2024, https://www.feverbee.com/different-types-of-communities/.

65   Donelson R. Forsyth, *Group Dynamics*, 5th ed. (Belmont, CA: Cengage Learning, 2010).

66   William W. Maddux and Marilynn B. Brewer, "Gender Differences in the Relational and Collective Bases for Trust," *Group Processes and Intergroup Relations* 8, no. 2 (2005): 159–171.

67   Shira Gabriel and Wendi L. Gardner, *Journal of Personality and Social Psychology* 87, no. 3 (2004): 423–435, https://doi.org/10.1037/0022-3514.87.3.423.

68   Émile Durkheim, "The Elementary Forms of Religious Life," translated by Joseph Ward Swain (London: George Allen & Unwin, 1915).

69   Lydia Denworth, "Brain Waves Synchronize when People Interact," *Scientific American*, May 9, 2023, https://www.scientificamerican.com/article/brain-waves-synchronize-when-people-interact/.

70   Daniel A. Yudkin, Annayah M. B. Prosser, S. Megan Heller, et al., "Prosocial Correlates of Transformative Experiences at Secular Multi-Day Mass Gatherings," *Nature Communications* 13 (2022), https://doi.org/10.1038/s41467-022-29600-1.

71   Ibid.

72   Douglas Belkin, "They Entered College in Isolation and Leave among Protests: The Class That Missed Out on Fun," *Wall Street Journal*, accessed April 26, 2024, https://www.wsj.com/us-news/education/college-fun-covid-pandemic-anxiety-ea992cee.

73   Jennifer L. Hirsch and Margaret S. Clark, "Multiple Paths to Belonging That We Should Study Together," *Perspectives on Psychological Science* 14, no. 2 (2019): 238–255, https://doi.org/10.1177/1745691618803629.

74   Esra Ascigil, Gul Gunaydin, Emre Selcuk, Gillian Sandstrom, and Erdal Aydin, "Minimal Social Interactions and Life Satisfaction: The Role of Greeting, Thanking, and Conversing," *Social Psychological and Personality Science*, December 4, 2023, 10:39.

75   Allie Contie, "Third Places: Where Americans Go to Meet New People after the Pandemic," *Atlantic*, April 2022, accessed April 30, 2024, https://www.theatlantic.com/family/archive/2022/04/third-places-meet-new-people-pandemic/629468/.

76   Ibid.

77   Jaye L. Derrick, Shira Gabriel, and Kurt Hugenberg, "Social Surrogacy: How Favored Television Programs Provide the Experience of Belonging," *Journal of Experimental Social Psychology* 45, no. 2 (2009): 352–362, https://doi.org/10.1016/j.jesp.2008.12.003.

78   Jordan D. Troisi and Shira Gabriel, "Chicken Soup Really Is Good for the Soul: 'Comfort Food' Fulfills the Need to Belong," *Psychological Science* 22, no. 6 (2011): 747–753, https://doi.org/10.1177/0956797611407931.

79   Mark Snyder, Ellen Berscheid, and Peter Glick, "Focusing on the Exterior and the Interior: Two Investigations of the Initiation of Personal Relationships," *Journal of Personality and Social Psychology* 48 (1985): 1427–1439.

80   Linchiat Chang and Robert M. Arkin, "Materialism as an Attempt to Cope with Uncertainty," *Psychology and Marketing* 19 (2002): 389–406.

81   Joel I. Norris, Nathaniel M. Lambert, C. Nathan DeWall, and Frank D. Fincham, "Can't Buy Me Love? Anxious Attachment and Materialistic Values," *Personality and Individual Differences* 53 (2012): 666–669.

82   Claudia Schulz, Hans-Helmut König, and André Hajek, "Differences in Self-Esteem Between Cat Owners, Dog Owners, and Individuals without Pets," *Frontiers in Psychology* 7 (September 2020), https://www.frontiersin.org/articles/10.3389/fpsyg.2021.759501/full:citation{index=0}.

83   Allen R. McConnell et al., "Friends with Benefits: On the Positive Consequences of Pet Ownership," *Journal of Personality and Social Psychology* 101, no. 6 (2011): 1239–1252, https://doi.org/10.1037/a0024506.

84   "Should You Pray to God? Sadhguru's Eye-Opening Answer,"
      YouTube, 6:58, May 19, 2020, accessed June 6, 2024, https://www.
      youtube.com/watch?v=VMVeZIAqcsA.

85   Chögyam Trungpa, *Cutting through Spiritual Materialism* (Boston:
      Shambhala Publications, 1973).

86   Stephanie Dorais and Daniel Gutierrez, "The Influence of Spiritual
      Transcendence on a Centering Meditation: A Growth Curve
      Analysis of Resilience," *Religions* 12, no. 8 (2021): 573, https://doi.
      org/10.3390/rel12080573.

87   James W. Pennebaker, "Expressive Writing and Health: Effects of
      Emotional Disclosure and Recounting Trauma," *Psychological Science*
      8, no. 3 (1997): 162–166.

88   Paul Stamets, interview by author, Boise, ID, June 6, 2024.

89   David B. Yaden, Jonathan Iwry, Kelley J. Slack, Johannes C. Eich-
      staedt, Yukun Zhao, George E. Vaillant, and Andrew B. Newberg,
      "The Overview Effect: Awe and Self-Transcendent Experience in
      Space Flight," *Psychology of Consciousness: Theory, Research, and
      Practice* 3, no. 1 (2016): 1–11.

90   Ray Dalio, "Life Principle: Realize That You Are Simultaneously
      Everything and Nothing—and Decide What You Want to Be,"
      Principles, last modified February 20, 2024, https://www.principles.
      com/principles/265acc65-c766-4200-a042-2a40753b1fce/.

91   Sonja Lyubomirsky, Kennon M. Sheldon, and David Schkade,
      "Pursuing Happiness: The Architecture of Sustainable Change,"
      Review of General Psychology 9, no. 2 (2005): 111–131.

92   James Currier, "Your Life Is Driven by Network Effects," February
      2020, https://www.nfx.com/post/your-life-network-effects.

93   Nicholas Lemann, "Kicking in Groups," *Atlantic*, April 1996,
      https://www.theatlantic.com/magazine/archive/1996/04/
      kicking-in-groups/376562/.

94   Scott Galloway (@profgalloway), "What's the most important decision you'll make in your life?" X (formerly Twitter), September 3, 2022, https://twitter.com/profgalloway/status/1566117931087429636.

95   Pew Research Center, "A Record High Share of Forty-Year-Olds in the US Have Never Been Married," June 28, 2023, https://www.pewresearch.org/short-reads/2023/06/28/a-record-high-share-of-40-year-olds-in-the-us-have-never-been-married/.

96   Derek Thompson, "Why Americans Care about Work So Much," *Atlantic*, March 31, 2023, accessed April 1, 2023, https://www.theatlantic.com/ideas/archive/2023/03/work-revolution-ai-wfh-new-book/673572/.

97   Bruce Feiler, *The Search: Finding Meaningful Work in a Post-Career World* (New York: Penguin Press, 2023).

98   Katherine Hamilton, "Want to Make a Friend? How Much Money Have You Got?" *Wall Street Journal*, May 17, 2024, https://www.wsj.com/personal-finance/making-friends-money-paid-activities-66d11144.

99   Michael A Singer, *The Untethered Soul: The Journey Beyond Yourself* (Oakland, CA: New Harbinger Publications, 2007).

100   David R. Hawkins, *Power versus Force: The Hidden Determinants of Human Behavior* (Carlsbad, CA: Hay House, 2002).

101   David R. Hawkins, "Map of Consciousness," *Power versus Force: The Hidden Determinants of Human Behavior* (Carlsbad, CA: Hay House, 2002).

102   Ibid.

103   Ray Dalio, *Principles: Life and Work* (New York: Simon & Schuster, 2017).

104   Edward R. Shapiro, "How Are They Right? A Way of Listening That Can Bridge Polarization," Ed Shapiro (blog), accessed April 6, 2024, https://www.edwardrshapiro.com/post/how-are-they-right-a-way-of-listening-that-can-bridge-polarization/.

105 Jeffrey A. Hall, "How Many Hours Does It Take to Make a Friend?" *Journal of Social and Personal Relationships* 36, no. 4 (2019): 1278–1296, https://doi.org/10.1177/0265407518761225.

106 Kelly-Ann Allen, Margaret L. Kern, Christopher S. Rozek, Dennis McInerney, and George M. Slavich, "Belonging: A Review of Conceptual Issues, an Integrative Framework, and Directions for Future Research," *Australian Journal of Psychology* 73, no. 1 (2021): 87–102, https://doi.org/10.1080/00049530.2021.1883409.

107 Will Guidara, *Unreasonable Hospitality: The Remarkable Power of Giving People More Than They Expect* (New York: Optimism Press, 2022), 7.

108 "Defining the Culture at Social Tables," Social Tables (blog), archived March 27, 2016, accessed May 2, 2024, https://web.archive.org/web/20160327183208/http://blog.socialtables.com/2012/07/19/defining-the-culture-at-social-tables/.

109 "Company Values, Part 1," Social Tables (blog), archived January 4, 2015, accessed May 2, 2024, https://web.archive.org/web/20150104234736/http://blog.socialtables.com/2013/11/06/company-values-part.

110 Geoffrey Cohen, *Belonging: The Science of Creating Connection and Bridging Divides* (New York: WW Norton & Company, 2022), 253.

111 Gallup, "The Increasing Importance of Having a Best Friend at Work," accessed May 2, 2024, https://www.gallup.com/workplace/397058/increasing-importance-best-friend-work.aspx.

112 "Workspaces That Move People," *Harvard Business Review*, accessed May 2, 2024, https://hbr.org/2014/10/workspaces-that-move-people.

INDEX

A

acceptance, 26
acquaintances, 122
agnosticism, 60
Allen, Kelly-Ann, 187–188
antidepressants, 84
anxious belonging, 90, 92, 144–145
anxious-preoccupied attachment, 78
Arendt, Hannah, 41
Aristotle, 109
atheism, 61
attachment style, 76–81, 213
attachment theory, 77

B

basecamp, 8, 51
belonging, 5–7, 9–10, 15–16, 213
    archetype, 76–77, 213
    Buttigieg on, 39–40
    crisis, 8, 39, 43, 213
    culture of, 195–198, 200–201
    defined, 21
    environment, 160–170, 213–214
    evolving conceptions of, 24
    as feedback loop, 24–26
    fit and, 24
    fuels, 66–69, 214
    hand-me-down, 70
    health and, 25
    identity *vs.*, 27–28
    integration of, into organizations, 205–210
    intentional, 140, 142–147
    loneliness and, 43–44
    in Maslow, 22
    mastering skills of, 180–187
    mindset, 214
    misconceived, 70–71
    as need, 21–24
    nontraditional fuels of, 67
    nostalgic, 70–71
    profile, 76–77
    as sense, 26–27
    storage for sense of, 65–66
    as story, 20
    subfuels of, 67
    taxonomy, 138–139
    on teams, 195–201
    traditional fuels of, 67
    as trendy, 21
    true, 29
    unintentional, 140
    workplace, 192–193
"blank slate," 56–57
bonds, symbolic, 126–128, 145–147, 209–210
book club, 116
Bowling Alone (Putnam), 35